McQueen Accounting Monograph Series
University of Arkansas – Fayetteville

Editor

Leon E. Hay, Ph.D., CPA
McQueen Distinguished Professor of Accounting

University of Arkansas – Fayetteville

McQueen Accounting Monograph Series

1. *Accounting: A Library of Quantifications*, by Stanley C. W. Salvary.

2. *Preliminary Evidence Regarding the Transfer Function Relationship of Quarterly Earnings for Closely-Related Industries*, by Clarence E. Fries.

ACCOUNTING:
A LIBRARY OF QUANTIFICATIONS

ACCOUNTING:
A LIBRARY OF QUANTIFICATIONS

(Theory Formulation Problems in Accounting)

by Stanley C. W. Salvary
Canisius College

University of Arkansas – Fayetteville
McQueen Accounting Monograph Series

ISBN 0-935951-00-8
Library of Congress Catalog Card No. 85-24543

Printed in the United States of America

Foreword

Publication of monographs in the McQueen Accounting Monograph Series is financed by income from the endowment of the Ralph L. McQueen Distinguished Chair of Accounting. Publication in the Series is available to any person or persons whose manuscript is judged to be of appropriate merit by referees known to be expert in the subject matter of the manuscript or in the research methodology utilized by the author(s). Manuscripts in any field of accounting, or in fields related to accounting, will be considered for publication in the McQueen Accounting Monograph Series.

The editor of the Series, and the author of this monograph, Professor Stanley C. W. Salvary of Canisius College, appreciate the time and thought given generously by members of the Faculty of the College of Business Administration of the University of Arkansas and by Theodore J. Mock, Arthur Andersen Alumni Professor of Accounting, University of Southern California, who reviewed the manuscript. The editor and author are particularly indebted to Robert R. Sterling, Kendall D. Garff Professor of Business Enterprise, University of Utah, who spent many hours in reviewing the manuscript of **Accounting: A Library of Quantifications** and in suggesting refinements to the manuscript.

Leon E. Hay
Editor, McQueen Accounting
Monograph Series

September 1985

Preface

This paper focuses on the major problem in accounting theory development which is the development of subsystems (sub-theories) under the guise of being the general theory. This paper attempts to demonstrate that these sub-theories are an integral part of the general theory. The integration of these sub-theories is not a contrived integration. These sub-theories are an inherent part of the general theory of accounting; they fit logically into a neat concept: **a library of systemic quantifications**. The main problem posed by these sub-theories is that they either reflect: (1) the limited view of accounting as the handmaiden of business; (2) the behavioral expectations of individuals in light of accounting information; (3) the failure to recognize the boundaries of accounting; and (4) the desire to transform the accounting information model into a decision model—attempting to internalize externalities.

The systems devised by some of these theorists (e.g. Chambers, Limperg and Sterling) are autonomous entities of internal dependencies (i.e. Continuously Contemporary Accounting, Replacement Value Accounting and Exit Value Accounting). Each approach of such theorists is a significant contribution as a matter of experimentation and in context of the framework of managerial accounting; however, when placed in context of the framework of financial accounting each approach appears to be a methodological decision which goes counter to zero-sum game accounting—the accounting for risk-sharing arrangements: the amount of the economic or social benefit (or burden) and how it is to be shared. The task at hand is to demonstrate that when accounting is viewed as an administrative information science for control and planning these functional models are special cases of the general case.

This paper is an analysis of those sub-theories culminating in an integration of these sub-theories into a general theory. It addresses the literature that those theorists generate on the basis of their models which are rigidly extrapolated from the conditions of their functioning. Those models are evidence of the generative aspects of accounting; however, such literature, which treats (assumes) each special case as the general case of accounting, creates an apparent antinomy that accounting information is decision-oriented and at the same time **not** decision-oriented because the duality of accounting (the difference between general information and decision-making information) is either not recognized or not appreciated.

I am indeed indebted to the many authors, in particular Professor Raymond J. Chambers and Professor Robert R. Sterling, whose works have stimulated my thinking and posed a challenge to me to write this monograph. I am also indebted to Professor Sterling for the many valuable comments. Additionally, I wish to acknowledge the many useful comments received from the anonymous reviewers and the editor.

This monograph is dedicated to my wife and children.

Stanley C. W. Salvary

Contents

List of Diagrams and Tables

I

INTRODUCTION

> *Interpretation. . .is the work of thought which consists in deciphering the hidden meaning in the apparent meaning, in unfolding the levels of meaning implied in the literal meaning.*
> (E)ach interpretation ... 'translates' the symbol according to its own frame of reference. (Ricoeur, 1974, pp. 13-14.)

Apparently, attempts at the development of a general theory of accounting have been foiled due to the lack of a unifying concept. This monograph introduces a unifying concept which is **Accounting: A Library of Quantifications.** This concept provides a framework for integrating the various special cases (sub-theories) of the general theory into a cohesive theory: a general theory of accounting.

Accounting is an adaptive mechanism adopted by society to help it to administer its affairs. As an adaptive mechanism, accounting is generative. Viewed in this context, accounting emerges as a **library of quantifications.** The term library is used herein to unify a diversified set of accounting models, which otherwise could be perceived as a divisive approach to the development of a scientific body of knowledge. The library approach signifies that as knowledge is discovered, on both the practical and theoretical planes, such information is stored for the purpose of reference and is made available for use, if and when needed. However, the type of information selected at any given time is dictated by circumstances at hand.

In accounting, the search and discovery of knowledge is a slow, but continuous, process. Nevertheless, the additions of quantifications, the storing of and subsequent availability of such information reflect the developmental process in accounting. In the search and discovery process, a quantification (derivable from a variety of quantification processes) is generated as needed to meet specific purposes, e.g., decision-making versus risk-sharing. These quantifications are complementary and are not contradictory, e.g., general information models versus decision-specific models. However, there are apparent contradictions when such quantifications are not viewed within this concept of accounting: a library (or portfolio) of quantifications. The objective of this monograph is to place in perspective the various models (e.g., exit value, entry value, and present value) so that the generative aspect of accounting can be appreciated. **The comments directed at the various models are not intended to diminish their importance but rather to establish the file in the library (or portfolio) to which they belong.** In so doing a general theory can be formalized.

II

Accounting Duality And Structural Concepts

Accounting duality refers not to the duality of transactions and events which are captured in a double-entry system of bookkeeping, but to the duality of accounting information. The accounting approach to information should not be viewed as monistic, but rather as dualistic. This view of accounting is predicated on the social evolutionary process.

Accompanying the evolution of the social system, there has been an evolution of a dualistic model of accounting. This dualistic model has made accounting more flexible in dealing with human action. Thus, the general theory of accounting must recognize and explicate the dualistic model of accounting. The dual aspects of the model are: feedback information for control in financial accounting which provides for risk-sharing arrangement by generating risk/return **performance** data; and feedforward and feedback information for planning in managerial accounting which provides for decision-making by projecting and evaluating risk/return **acceptance** data.

To explore the implication of the dualistic model it is necessary to focus on the interrelationship between accounting and society. This interrelationship can best be described using three structural concepts borrowed from but not used in the same manner as Karl R. Popper (1972, pp. 276-279). These concepts are: (1) the central propensity structure of the socio-economic system; (2) the controlled executive structure of the socio-economic system; and (3) the aim-structure of the accounting (discipline) system. Popper (1972) used those terms in relation to a biological setting, whereas, as used herein, the terms are used in a social evolutionary context. The use of structural concepts is to provide an analytical framework within the social evolutionary process. The central propensity structure is the concern for control and planning of human behavior in an organized setting – this feature is essentially the role of administration. The controlled executive structure is the concern for the institutions that would constitute the framework within which human action shall be conducted – this feature is institutional arrangement. The aim-structure is essentially the function of accounting within the context of the institutional arrangement that would facilitate the role of administration.

Changes in the environment over time (e.g., from a public economy in Sumer to a significant private sector economy with capital markets) favored the sharpening of focus of the aim-structure of accounting. The sharpening of focus resulted in a division of focus thus making explicit the dualistic model of accounting. With the monetization of the economy (the replacement of a barter economy with a money exchange economy), the measure of exchange became the means of payment. The physical unit was no longer the basis of recording, instead a uniform nominal money value became the dominant basis of recording; the physical unit remained as a subsidiary measure. Two branches of accounting became explicit: financial accounting emerged explicitly to deal with risk-sharing arrangement pertaining to the unit – the money raising entity (Shannon, 1954, p. 358); whereas managerial accounting emerged explicitly to deal with the unit as a series of subsystems and events as viewed from a variety of possible states of nature. All types of accounting units (business, government and philanthropy) were recognized in this process.

Before the emergence of the dualistic model, many varied valuations have been used in accounting (Winjum, 1970, p. 758; 1972, pp. 85, 208). This condition suggests that accounting can be viewed as a library or portfolio of quantifications. The library concept of accounting is differentiable from both: (a) the multi-columnar presentation of alternative accounting valuations alongside each other, and (b) the concept of 'a different measure of income for different purposes'. With regard to (a), the library concept maintains that as valuations are discovered by experimentation, they are stored for use as circumstances would warrant. With regard to (b), the library concept maintains that **in the general case** the various valuations are needed as composite parts to form a complete picture of observed phenomena. It is only in the special case that one measure would provide the complete picture.

As a library, accounting has the capacity to extend itself to accommodate changes in the environment – either in the central propensity structure or in the controlled structure. For instance, the emergence of the investment company (a company organized for the express purpose of acquiring and managing a portfolio of debt and equity securities) produced a change in the controlled structure. Since the circumstances of the investment company are unlike those of manufacturing and other financial companies (banks and insurance companies), a search of the files in the library was undertaken to identify the accounting for investment companies. Valuation is circumstantial or situational, thus the valuation which best fits (describes) the circumstances is chosen. In this case it was realizable value.

Many attempts at revising or reconstructing accounting theory have focused unfortunately on certain dimensions of accounting and not on its totality. This condition has plagued and yet enhanced the development of accounting theory. A neat and concise though not all-inclusive summary is to bc found in the American Accounting Association Committee on Concepts and Standards for External Financial Reports' *Statement on Accounting Theory and Theory Acceptance* (1977). Present problems encountered in the development of a structurally sound theory of accounting are in part due to the attempts to substitute a sub-theory for the general theory. Though not recognizing the various theories as sub-theories of a general theory of accounting but rather as competing theories of a general theory of accounting, the American Accounting Association Committee (1977) writing the aforementioned report indicated that none of the proponents of those competing theories was able to establish the ascendancy of any one theory over all the others. Some of these sub-theories are embodied in the following broad categories of interpretation:

1) A Limited View of Accounting as the Handmaiden of Business
2) A Predisposed Behavioral Expectation
3) A Failure to Recognize the Boundaries of Accounting
4) An Attempt to Internalize Externalities

Each interpretation in the search of a general theory of accounting is grounded in a particular existential function:

> [E]ach of the accounting approaches currently advocated involves a unique way of looking at the accounting problem at hand, whatever it may happen to be. Indeed *each approach tends to self-select the problems with which it will deal* as well as the means it will employ to attack these problems. (American Accounting Association, 1977, p. 43) (Emphasis added)

This monograph attempts to identify the nature of the subtheories enumerated, examine their underlying rationale as expounded by the major advocates, and then integrate them into a general theory.[1]

[1]This point has been observed or at least intimated by Mattessich. (1964, p. 8).

III

Sub-Theories: Phenomenological Interpretations

Essentially, each sub-theory constitutes an interpretation of a phenomenological nature involving a spatio-temporally ordered system of observable money and commodity flows which are influenced by technology and taste. Each theory translates phenomena according to its particular frame of reference. Such frames of reference now become the subject of discussion.

A Limited View of Accounting as the Handmaiden of Business

Theorists such as Littleton and Zimmerman (1962, p. 79) [along with Edwards and Bell (1961, pp. 6, 7) among others] have maintained that: "Accounting had been developed by and for private enterprise. Its primary service had been and still is to aid management." Chambers (1966, p. 61) maintains: "Accounting is concerned with commercial experiences, events and considerations." However, like Paton (1922, pp. 16-27), he is explicit concerning the broader implications of accounting:

> I wished to leave in no doubt my concern with specific particulars, the consideration of which, alone, can yield grounds for belief and tests of belief in one kind of accounting or another. (Chambers, 1966, p. 15)

On the other hand, Williams and Griffin (1964, p. 220) make the disclaimer: "business does not have the right to claim for itself all the capacities of accounting." Whereas, Ijiri (1971, p. 3) maintains that: accounting is a system for communicating economic events of an entity. There are very few exceptions to the view that accounting is the handmaiden of business. Two notable exceptions are Moonitz (1961, pp. 4-5) and Wheeler (1971, p. 27). According to Wheeler (1971, p. 27):

> Accounting. . .is not the handmaiden of business, and it is not the role of accountants to preserve any particular institution or specific economic system. Accounting is a universal type of information system which is needed in every known form of economic system and by all resource-using people or organizations within these systems. In our own society, accounting is vital to government as to business, to non-profit organizations as to business firms. We need to expand our horizons but not so much in terms of a larger role within the business firm but rather to a larger role within society by giving more attention to our possible service to non-business organizations and to society in general.

According to Wheeler's line of reasoning accounting is not peculiar to, but rather is responsive to any system, therefore accounting is not identifiable with a particular system but with all (the many and diverse) systems. Accounting is therefore dispassionate.

For the purpose of analysis in this paper, it is necessary: (1) to dispel this limited view of accounting as the handmaiden of business, and (2) to demonstrate that accounting should be viewed as an administrative information science which of necessity is dispassionate in order that its underlying principles be universally applicable. Accordingly, it is postulated that a delimited field of attributes exists anterior to the constitution of an accounting framework. This field of attributes is anterior to objectivity for accounting measurement. Before objectivity, there is the horizon of the socio-economic system; before measurement as formulated in the theory of accounting, there is administrative life; **the accounting measurement is derived from administrative life.** This condition manifested itself in Sumerian civilization:

> [A]t Lagash, . . . scribes record without effort and without difficulty the incoming and outgoing (goods) of the Palace. . . .
>
> It suffices that at that period [of expanded human activity] a high ranking personnage, scribe by profession, had established by taste rather than by necessity, a system of written control . . . .

> [I]n order to mitigate a growing disorganization, those in charge . . . brought into their service some technical improvements in the sense of a greater control in the distribution of commodities . . .which had become rare. (Lambert, 1960, pp. 19-25. Translated by Dr. RoseAnne Martin)

In light of the foregoing, accounting emerged within the context of a collective effort. Thus, any attempt to generalize, from any theory of accounting built around the business enterprise, will run into difficulty. This condition will hold since it would be an attempt to force the general case into a specific case of the general case. Since accounting is derived from administrative life, it involves the planning and control of human behavior; however, it does not contradict social choice nor does it mean that human behavior is predisposed. Social choice implies that human beings as emotional creatures respond to stimuli (information); they behave in a manner most suitable to them within the existing constraints.

Predisposed behavior implies that human beings will behave in a certain manner given a certain stimulus (information); thus, human beings should be given information to produce a predetermined behavior from them. Social control operates from this latter premise, since the need for social control is based upon the desirability of certain established social values and the maintenance of such social values. However, when desirable social values are not at stake, but instead individuals' freedom to make choices (wise or foolish) is at stake, a danger exists in attempting to generate information so that behavior would be predetermined. Evidently, to generate information based upon the expectation that individuals would behave in a predisposed manner is an approach that challenges social choice, which is the cornerstone of society. Nevertheless, it seems that some theorists are inclined to believe that there exists in society an expectation for only a certain type of information.

Predisposed Behavioral Expectation

The evidence on accounting from an investigation of evolutionary stages and conditions of social adaptation precludes the generation of *a* type of information based upon predisposed behavioral expectations, but rather supports the need for and the generation of many types of information. As discernible from the general case, accounting information is situational; and as an information science, accounting is generative. It seems that a predisposed behavioral expectation approach flourishes in the absence of an historical investigation, and consequently it produces a special case of the general case.

In this school of thought (predisposed behavioral expectation), accounting information is viewed as decision specific. The decision-maker receiving the accounting information is said to be primarily concerned with the future, with little concern for what has transpired and why. This view of accounting is in conflict with: (1) the stewardship function of accounting, and (2) the fact or possibility that security owners (as one distinct group of decision-makers) may be much more interested in the reliability of management — basically a proven track record from the past. This concern of security owners does not negate their concern for what the management will do in the future; but it is fairly obvious that a past track record is a key factor in assessing the future potential of management.

Sterling (1970a), who is a leading exponent of this school of thought, recognizes the concern of investors for management's decision-making ability which can only be assessed from management's past performance. However, he seems to suppress this concern by showing preference for future prospects.

> The problematic situation that the trader and other interested receivers find themselves in is one of valuation. They need to make a decision that involves the ranking of goods. The ranking process requires a prediction of the future-state-of-being of the competing goods. (Sterling, 1970a, pp. 155-156)

Apparently, there is a clear need for information on past performance as differentiated from information on future prospects. This condition (dual need) made explicit the duality of accounting. Evidently to ignore the duality of accounting and to establish one area of accounting (decision-making information) as the totality of accounting is to attempt to transform the special case (predisposed behavioral expectation) into the general case. For example, Sterling (1970a), uses a special model as a basis for generalization.

> The criterion of relevance reduces to the specification of the problematic situation and the decision

> theory applicable to that situation. . . One requirement of all decision theories is that the available alternatives be specified. . .
>
> Past (purchase) prices have no relevance to any well-formulated decision theory that we are aware of. Such values are sunk and therefore cannot specify the currently available alternatives. . .
>
> *In short, the Present Market method of valuation is... relevant to all receivers,* because it specifies the currently available alternatives and the ability to perform current obligations. (Sterling, 1970a, pp. 358-360) (Emphasis added)

The preceding passage reveals a focus on a non-zero-sum game: planning to maximize returns (the realm of managerial accounting — a decision-making orientation); and not on a zero-sum game: agreeing on how risk and return will be shared (the realm of financial accounting — a control orientation). Essentially the approach cited above assumes a monistic role for accounting information, and consequently, the special case is treated as the general case. It is quite clear in the accounting literature that the problems of a monistic approach are many:

> The complexity of factors influencing decision-making in many situations has severely limited the application of many of these normative procedures. . . .[A] single-minded preoccupation with the evaluation of alternative courses of action also raises a number of problems. For one thing, . . . [some theorists] rarely consider the means by which the alternatives are to be generated and their concern with evaluation presumes values. Yet it is possible that the value premises inherent in the decision procedures differ radically from those of the decision-makers for whom they are intended.
>
> A comprehensive understanding of the process by which people actually make decisions, and of what influences them in these endeavours, is therefore essential for a more effective utilization of normative decision models. (Hopwood, 1974, p. 123)
>
> Diversity among the type of decisions that must be made, complicated and unknown goal hierarchies. . .

> Our limited knowledge and imperfect understanding of decision problems prevent us from identifying common elements or basic principles underlying accounting measurements to be provided for such general, vague problems. (Jensen, 1971, p.38)

Even within a decision-making context one finds variation in motives; hence, the relevant information would seemingly differ based upon the variation in motives. Consequently, any functional model of financial accounting constructed with a decision orientation would be subject to the following comment:

> ...[It] would ... [be preferable] to view the theory-building process in accounting as a process of observing masses of scientific observations from decision environments and thought processes of managers, investors, and government officials. Perhaps there are common elements that can be related to the common elements of certain existing or proposed accounting processes. Only then can theorists effectively guide policy formulation in accounting on the basis of evidence of systematic, scientific observations which are relevant. . .
>
> Accounting, we would agree, is intended to 'serve' decision-makers. Accordingly, 'local rules' must differ in serving decision-makers along a continuum between economic man and the Burmese businessman who according to Miller and Starr, prefers the pleasure of bargaining to the achievement of profit. (Jensen, 1971, p. 40)

General Knowledge and Decision-Making Information. It is quite true that if accounting is to be useful it must serve decision-makers, but *it does not mean that the totality of accounting must be decision-making oriented*. Accordingly, as an information science, accounting should be viewed as being truly information oriented. Since it is not a science of choice, accounting is not limited to the generation of information for decision-making only; accordingly, it incorporates information in the sense of general knowledge. A difference does exist between general knowledge and decision-making information, although at times some information may be uniquely appropriate for satisfying both types of information needs. Under such circumstances a monistic approach to measurement is justifiable, but in general a monistic approach to information is inappropriate. In this regard, both Chambers (1966, pp. 91, 351) and Sterling (1970a, pp. 358-360) take a monistic approach to accounting measurement. In Chambers' and Sterling's defense, it must be pointed out that in a socio-economic system in which physical quantities are the only relevant magnitudes and the system of exchange is based upon custom and not competition, the accounting library is reduced to a single valuation — physical quantities. This point can be inferred from the following:

> In ancient Egypt, as elsewhere in early times, the use of money was unknown, *and the fiscal receipts and payments of Pharaoh were in kind*. . . The royal treasury partook of the character of the farm, the warehouse, and the manufactory. (Boyd, 1905, p. 20) (Emphasis added)

Since modern economies are characterized by a different institutional setting from the setting above, it would appear that the monistic approach of Chambers and Sterling ignores the "controlled executive structure" of the socio-economic system. This condition is essentially the failure to recognize or accept the dualistic model of accounting; it is a failure to recognize that their models for decision-making are special cases of the general case. Since decision-making information is only one of the two major reference files (financial accounting and managerial accounting), with each major file containing several sub-files, their models cannot be assumed to be general models of accounting.[2] Therefore, it is necessary to stress that their models belong to the managerial accounting reference file in the library of quantifications.

The reason for such classification in the reference file of managerial accounting and not in the other major reference file of financial accounting is fairly obvious. Financial accounting is not an evaluative (future oriented) model because it is primarily a feedback (control) model, whereas, managerial accounting is primarily a feedforward (planning) model. However, these two theorists allow evaluation into the framework of financial accounting (they consider their models as being financial accounting

[2]For instance Mattesich (1964, pp. 9, 18) does recognize the difference in information types.

models). Presumably, they see no need for a separation between the control and planning functions of accounting within the context of an information model. However, there exists a clear distinction between the control (risk-sharing) function of financial accounting and the planning (decision-making) function of managerial accounting. The following passages serve to illustrate the distinction from an historical perspective. The control function and role of feedback data as *input* into the decision-making (planning) process are implied by the following:

> An elaborate system of account-keeping was required *for the recording and for the planning based on it*. Income and expenditures were scrupulously drawn up with summary balance statements by the officials of the separate districts. They were forwarded to the king's official in Ur, and so each year the agricultural yield could be planned. (Roebuck, 1966, p. 35) (Emphasis added)

The planning function may be perceived through the following actions:

> Pericles [in 461 B.C.], himself a landowner [and a manorial administrator], organized his own estates according to the principles of commercial logic. For example, he confounded the conservatives by selling the produce of his own land and purchasing food in the market. (Gordon, 1975, p. 12)

> Each year the reeve disposed [of the skins] for a fair sum . . . while if the sheep were struck by murrain before the shearing, the wool still fetched its price. Even the carcases on occasion were sold, presumably to be used for tallow. The minuteness of the work of a medieval reeve is particularly evident *in studying his accountancy and realising the careful planning that must have lain behind these sales, and the care taken to utilise every possible source of revenue*. The entry in 1308 of the receipt of 2d. for peacock's feathers is a classic example. (Page, 1936, p. xxx) (Emphasis added)

The foregoing illustrations serve to emphasize the general information approach of financial accounting and the information evaluation approach of managerial accounting. Apparently, financial accounting information provides a basis for evaluation when placed in context with other information. However, it is managerial accounting that is the evaluative mechanism for decision-making.

Predictive Ability. The distinction becomes clearer when one considers predictive ability as related to financial accounting theory as opposed to the nature of the predictive ability for managerial accounting. The predictive ability for the former is concerned with explanation; whereas, for the latter the concern is with projection (Mattesich, 1964, pp. 20, 237). The distinction between the two is that the former (explanation) provides a basis for scientific understanding; whereas, the latter (projection) merely provides a basis for administrative policy: simply, ''If it works let's use it — it really does not matter if we do not understand why it works.'' Since a theory is supposed to provide an explanation and possibly aid in predicting the future, to accept projection as the equal of explanation will cast serious doubts on the validity of any theory claiming scientific import. Unfortunately, projection has been accepted as adequate support for financial accounting theory.

> It is not necessary that the postulates be true or even realistic. . . The assumptions that provide the greatest degree of prediction may be more useful than those that are most realistic. (Hendriksen, 1982, p. 61)

This position has been rejected by many theorists in other disciplines, including Basmann (1972), Hanna (1972), and Morgenstern (1963, pp. 92-98). Essentially the basis of such rejection, which is equally applicable in accounting, is that from a scientific standing the ability to predict without being able to explain (describe the behavior) is worthless (Leibenstein, 1976, p. 13); it is only when predictions arise from coherent and communicable explanations that they are of any value from a scientific standpoint.

Beaver, et al (1968, pp. 678-680) discuss the predictive ability criterion, however, their concern is projection in context of decision-making, i.e., forecasting (the best statistical fit of ex ante data to ex post data), and thus seemingly settle for statistical goodness of fit instead of explanation (operational characteristics) of the phenomena. When the concern is for a policy on investment decisions, then a linear model with variables tested to select those producing the best fit (prediction) is adequate. It is necessary to draw the distinction between forecasting the future and prediction, which is essentially deducing an occurrence in a timeless setting from initial conditions. It is for this reason, the desire to deduce from an explanation, that the "aim-structure" of accounting has been divided so that managerial accounting would permit hypothesis formulation and testing. It is, therefore, in this latter sense that managerial accounting accommodates decision-making. Yet, the practical side of managerial policy cannot and is not being disputed here: the role of forecasting as a matter of managerial policy is embedded in the intuitive aspect of decision-making.

The concern is for the grounding of accounting theory as a scientific theory. Since a description of observed phenomena serves as a basis for understanding the phenomena, it in effect is an explanation of the phenomena though it may not permit of prediction. However, there is a strong link between explanation and prediction, in that explanation provides the foundation for prediction.[3] Nevertheless, a scientific theory can have an explanatory power and a predictive power; *while a scientific theory may lack predictive power, it may not lack explanatory power* (Leibenstein, 1976, p. 13).

Theoretical Realism. Explanation requires theoretical realism. For explanation as a condition in financial accounting to satisfy theoretical realism, financial accounting information would be required to truly describe, and not necessarily predict, the *actual behavior* of units in markets. As stated earlier, when the term explanation is used as a synonym for evaluation and projection – (both of which are very useful for pragmatic managerial policy), explanation merely requires a statistical goodness of fit and therefore does not satisfy the requirements of a theory. *However in the accounting discipline, managerial accounting* (since it draws upon the *explanatory* power of financial accounting) is vested with some predictive power, and accordingly *does permit prediction based upon induction* (from financial statements) *and subsequent deduction* (in budgets). Apparently, accounting theory possesses, in context of the dual "aim structure" of accounting, both explanatory and predictive powers.

---

[3]For a lucid discussion of the relationship between explanation and prediction, and of the significance of explanation, see Popper (1972, pp. 349-361).

One final point which requires mention in this section is that the two major reference files in accounting are guided by two distinct, though related, theoretical frameworks: a risk-sharing perspective in the case of financial accounting; and a decision-making perspective in the case of managerial accounting. These two perspectives on data collection and processing which consitute the field of accounting do not exhaust the field of information. Accounting information is a limited information set, although some theorists may claim a greater (and even a limitless) capacity for accounting. They recognize no limitations or boundaries to the accounting discipline. This condition is the basis of the next area of discussion.

Failure to Recognize the Boundaries of Accounting

Certain sub-theories (Sweeney, 1936; MacNeal 1939) view accounting as essentially without boundaries. Boundaries are established in each discipline to insure full development of each discipline at those points of intersection with other formal disciplines. This condition is present in the case of chemistry vs physics; medicine vs psychology.[4] Recognition of the points of intersection of one discipline with other disciplines is very important, since such recognition would enable an understanding of the usefulness of findings in other disciplines to the discipline under consideration. Also of great importance is the recognition of the differences in scope and mission of the various disciplines in order to avoid confusion in focus. Once boundaries are established the observations making up the data source for that discipline are limited in order to avoid unnecessary duplication. The limitation is not one of the capacity of the discipline to deal with problems, but of what constitutes the discipline. The discipline must be definable.

[4]For instance: "Psychoanalysis ... sees only one dimension of the symbol: the dimension in which symbols are seen as derivations of repressed desires. ...[I]t cannot be reproached for this narrowness; it is its raison d'être. Pschoanalysis can find only what it seeks ... [and] thus... [is] unable to find anything other than the disguised expressions of representations and affects (sic) belonging to the most archaic of man's desires." Ricoeur (1974, pp. 14-15).

Boundary Conditions. Limitations which are due to *boundary* conditions of a discipline are different in nature and impact from limitations due to *deficiency* conditions of a discipline. The latter is a failure of the discipline, and every attempt should be made to rid the discipline of such deficiencies. Whereas, limitations due to boundary conditions of the discipline in no manner reflect a failure of the discipline. When the term limitation(s) is used in the subsequent discussion it signifies *boundary conditions* and not *deficiency conditions*. The literature in economics and finance constitute food for thought; however, accountants have tried to make it accounting doctrine. Littleton (1970) is most outspoken on this issue of the recognition of the limitation of accounting. On the other hand, Shwayder (1971) has stressed that accountants should not allow "superficial similarities" to obscure "subtle differences" between accounting and economics.[5]

Prescriptive and Descriptive Systems. For a normative (prescriptive) system, as is the case in economics, simplifying assumptions are used and quantifications along those lines are used. This approach is both legitimate and useful. However, when a positive (descriptive) system is involved as in the case with financial accounting (which entails information generation and dissemination processes) the quantifications so chosen are to be based upon concepts which should correspond with the structures and the regularities of the system which has been described. Underlying Sweeney's (1936) quantification, for reforming financial accounting, is the concept of **real capital**. "Real capital" is derived from the general concept: **calculate in "real" terms**. To calculate in real terms (real income, real capital), there is need to arrive at a "real" money. For purposes of this discussion, a "real" dollar is substituted for "real" money.

A "real" dollar does not exist; only a "nominal" dollar exists. A "real" dollar is a nominal dollar divided by the general price index. (Friedman and Schwartz, 1982, p. 17) The "real" dollar concept is based upon the implied constancy of consumers' want-satisfaction over time. This is a simplistic assumption adopted for the purpose of interperiod *physical quantity* comparisons for a

[5]Chambers (1966, pp. 351-371) and Mattesich (1964, p. 235) have also emphasized the difference between accounting and economics.

given economy and for intraperiod *physical quantity* comparisons among several economies. (Kravis, 1984, p. 3) The ''real'' dollar (''real'' income, ''real'' capital) concept is an attempt to translate financial expenditures into a physical quantity flow. (Kravis, 1984, pp. 2,3)

It is the concern for physical quantity comparisons that gives rise to the concept of ''real'' term calculation. This physical quantity comparability was the area of concern for Fritz Schmidt (whose work influenced Sweeney) in Germany after World War I, and for policy-makers in France for the purpose of planning national output. (Sweeney, 1936, pp. 8, 40-42; Enthoven, 1973, p. 302) However, it is certainly not related to risk-sharing arrangements within and among the users and suppliers of resources in a **money economy** in which case exchange-value in nominal terms predominates. The aggregate expenditure on each item reflects consumers' choices; and a physical quantity in one period may not be equally desirable in another, simply because of a change in taste.

Financial accounting as a descriptive system is concerned with want-satisfaction which is captured in financial terms and not in physical units. Nominal money is the legitimate means of expressing want-satisfaction in a money economy. Stephens (1967, p. 62) implicitly recognized both the distinction and the interdependence of the physical quantity system and the financial (money price) system. He maintained that there are those persons who seem to believe that the measurable quantum is the physical quantity of goods, while overlooking the nature of or the satisfaction generated by the goods.

Simplifying Assumptions vs Necessary Conditions. Underlying MacNeal's (1939) concern for reform of financial accounting is the concept of the 'adequacy of disclosure', (e.g. management's plans, intended sale of significant assets, etc.) The disclosure issue was turned into a valuation issue by MacNeal's (1939, pp. 102, 147, 181) call for the use of economic values in place of accounting values. Economic values are useful for their intended purposes; they do not serve all purposes. The usefulness of economic values does not mean that those values are substitutable for accounting values. For instance, the question may be asked for the purpose of inter-country comparison: What is the value of the financial instruments (e.g. companies' shares) that are traded in each of the capital markets of the countries under observation? The economic value of the financial instruments would be arrived at by taking the aggregate shares of each company (whose shares are traded in the respective markets) and pricing them out using the current market prices (the unit prices that obtained on the last trade of each company's shares) as of the given date of the observation.

The market value arrived at for the financial instruments of each country is not the amount of money that would be exchanged for those financial instruments. To assume that this aggregate value would prevail if all those financial instruments were brought to market all at once, it would mean that a necessary condition (the law of supply and demand) of the market place is assumed not to be operative. To maintain that the aggregate market value would obtain, an implicit assumption would exist. That is the unit prices of the last trades, which were experienced for a limited supply (a small quantity) of the financial instruments, would be the same unit prices that would be experienced immediately thereafter for an unlimited supply (the entire quantity) of the financial instruments. This condition would be the substitution of necessary conditions underlying market price with a simplifying assumption about market price.

For a limited number of entities, which arc financial intermediaries and trade daily in the capital market (e.g. investment companies), the use of current market is appropriate. However, for all entities with securities portfolios which would constitute a larger supply of financial instruments, it would be contrary to fact to maintain that the last traded market price or an amount reasonably close to it would prevail. MacNeal's (1939) concern for disclosure (the use of inside information by a few at the expense of the investing public) is valid. Disclosure of market values of securities portfolios indicating the potential for gain and post balance sheet disclosures of significant events have become standard disclosures in financial statements.

Under MacNeal's approach, the necessary conditions for measurement in a descriptive (positive) system are treated as simplifying assumptions of a prescriptive (normative) system.

Simplfying assumptions are the removal of reality for the purpose of developing a means of analysis fully cognizant of the limitations. In financial accounting the going-concern assumption is in reality a necessary set of conditions: (1) Financial solvency or demonstrated operating financing or program funding ability; (2) a marketable product or program for an existing market or constituency; and (3) the existence and execution of plans for the production, marketing and distribution/delivery of the product or program. These conditions *are not assumed to exist but in fact must exist* for financial accounting measurement to be applied. When the set of conditions is satisfied, it justifies the use of the estimated recoverable cost (committed money) approach as opposed to the liquidation or exit value approach to measurement.

The going-concern implies the future, and future signifies uncertainty. It is with regard to uncertainty that the concept of realization emerges. Realization is a quality control principle: by reducing the uncertainty in the quantification process to an acceptable level, it insures equity among the suppliers of resources. It is the concept of equity which underlies the realization principle in financial accounting.

Abstraction of reality does not mean idealization of reality. What is appropriate for economics is not necessarily appropriate for accounting. The disclosure problem is a financial reporting problem, and hence it is a much broader issue than the disclosure requirements for financial accounting information. At present, there exists a deficiency in accounting disclosure. Managerial accounting information (budgets, forecasts, etc.) should be provided to users of financial reports, but such information generally is not made available. Eventually, such disclosures will be made as management's reluctance to disclose that type of information is overcome (such was the case with segment information).

It does not matter how extensive accounting information happens to be, there still exist many bits of information of a non-accounting nature which are desirable to provide a more complete picture of the entity (e.g. trade statistics, technological advances in an industry, etc.). The fact that these added statistical and other data are desirable is in no manner a reflection of a deficiency condition in accounting, but it merely reflects the boundary conditions in accounting.

To reinforce the concept of boundary as applied to accounting, an analogy can be drawn between accounting and chemistry. If chemistry concerns itself with the composition (properties) of certain objects, and physics in general, though not in all cases, concerns itself with the relation of those same objects over time and space (Guerlac, 1961, pp. 64-68), similarly, accounting identifies the composition (as reflected in monetary transactions) of oganizations, while economics attempts to assess behavior (assign optimum values) to those organizations over time and space (markets).

The analogy, for the purpose of establishing the limitations (due to boundary conditions) of accounting, can be better understood in light of biological and psychological reports. The assignment of certain values by the physician to an individual who has been submitted to a thorough physical examination is in no manner comparable to the assignment of the values contained in the psychoanalytical report, prepared by the psychoanalyst concerning the same individual. The medical report identifies certain properties; whereas, the psychoanalytical report concern itself with the individual in relation to time and environment. Those (biological and psychological) reports are produced as a matter of information for the individual, and at other times, particularly in the case of employment, for decision-makers (employers and prospective employers). In the hands of the individual such reports reflect general knowledge about the individual; whereas, in the hands of a decision-maker (e.g., an employer) such information is transformed into data for the specific purpose at hand. When such general knowledge is used for evaluating the employment potential of an individual, it is the employer or prospective employer who ultimately assigns a value (score or ranking based upon the organization's own scale of measurement for such purposes) which is derived from the employer's or prospective employer's decision model.

The Accounting Measurement Unit as a Linear Measure. Furthermore, any measure is subject to some type of limitation, e.g. length versus volume. Linear measures (foot, yard) differ from measures of volume (cubic foot, cubic yard). The unit of measurement used in accounting is unidimensional; thus, it is more like a linear measure than a volume measure.[6] Hence, this limitation of the accounting measurement unit, the monetary expression which is an unidimensional measure, must be recognized and accepted as such.

[6]The distance analogy as applied to monetary measure in a money economy can be appreciated following an outline developed in physics. Accordingly:

$$\text{Miles Travelled} = X \frac{\text{miles}}{\text{hour}} \cdot Y \text{ Hours}$$

or

$$\text{Distance} = \text{Velocity} \cdot \text{Time}$$

To appreciate the linear measure analogy, one must recognize that it is exchange value that is being measured when a transaction takes place; and exchange value reflects the conditions under which a particular transaction has occurred. Exchange value is a dynamic value and not a constant value; since it captures the dynamics of the system, it reflects a market economy guided by prices. In a money economy, it is money which is used to measure exchange value. Money being the measurement device simply provides a nominal value (**price**) which reflects the allocation process (Eiriksson, 1954, p. 351; Arrow, 1974, p. 20). **Prices** of all goods and services can be uniformly expressed in the system because of the money measure. On the other hand volume measures (which are expressed in a wide variety of physical unit measures) are provided for in the system — statistics on units of output (production levels) are disseminated by government agencies and trade organizations.

An extremely good understanding of the accounting measurement process is provided by Johnson (1954, p. 246):

> [T]he distinction between value and valuation is...a useful one. [V]aluation . . . means only that a useful relationship has been established between the monetary unit and some element of property and property rights. Valuation in this context must be judged primarily on the basis of its usefulness — if it serves well the purpose for which it is intended, and everyone understands that purpose, it is a useful valuation. The relationship between physical inventories and the

---

[6] (Continued)

For financial accounting, this concept emerges as follows:

$$\text{Money Exchanged} = X \frac{\text{Dollars}}{\text{Commodity}} \cdot Y \text{ Commodities}$$

or

$$\text{Value} = \text{Price} \cdot \text{Physical Quantity}$$

According to Marion (1973, pp. 14-15): "This equation does not explicitly contain the units of the various quantities; the equation is valid for any system of units as long as the system is used consistently." It must be emphasized that it is valid for any system because both the numbers and the units must balance in the equation: Distance = XY miles; Value = XY dollars.

> monetary outlay necessary to bring them to their present status is a useful valuation, to be compared with a later selling price to establish a gain or loss. If the selling price turns out to be greater than expected, it may also be useful to determine that a speculative price gain has been realized as well as the normal operating margin. Thus a whole series of valuations may be used in accounting for economic events to furnish information to those concerned. The choice among methods of valuation rests not on any proof of correctness of one valuation over another — but questions of logic, usefulness, and measurability...

The position taken above is highly consistent with measurement theory:

> We can state conditions under which we are warranted in saying that a quantity exists or that a physical object is present. And this is not a metaphysical hypothesis, for it has empirical consequences . . . If we say that a certain quantity is present we will expect that certain relations (underlying circumstances) which we have shown to be approximately symmetrical and transitive (e.g., current assets) or asymmetrical and transitive (e.g., fixed assets) in a certain field (for an individual firm) will remain so in an extended field (for all firms confronted with similar/identical underlying circumstances). Moreover, we will expect to find other relations which generate more or less the same order, and yet others which lead to a more consistent ordering of things (Ellis, 1966, p. 37).

The foregoing holds true provided in accounting theory the assignment of numerals to items are in accordance with a determinative, non-degenerate rule. Thus, **the concept of distance** (a uni-dimension measure) as a measurable operation **is the measurement concept** underlying the monetary unit in accounting. This condition is so because when one measures the distance a vehicle has travelled by reading the vehicle's odometer at the beginning and end of the journey, one has no knowledge of how much weight (vehicle's content during the journey) was transported over the distance travelled. To obtain such information one must use another source other than the odometer, but this condition does not signify that the distance travelled is incorrect, nor that the measuring device is deficient. The attempt to get a volume measurement from a length measurement has "failed because of practical, technical problems of making a standard mass of specified linear dimensions." (Weatherall, 1968, p. 57)

It is imperative to recognize that **within a money economy** accounting is a valuation discipline that focuses on a money flow and not on a physical flow, although the physical flow does underlie the money flow. The volume/length measurement problem in physics finds its counterpart in accounting in the form of the physical/money flow. This measurement problem has to be solved in mathematics in a manner that is consistent with the physical science. As can be deduced, this limitation is not a failure of accounting. Accordingly, financial accounting does not arrive at intrinsic or real values but arrives at a valuation which is described, explaining effects in terms of money flow and the composition of such money flows.

Economics is the discipline that attempts to arrive at true values derivable from its laws of market processes and wealth accumulation. However, according to Canning (1929, pp. 197, 245-246) if that discipline which is concerned with true or real values cannot arrive at those values in any provable sense, why should accounting be forced to take on that responsibility? Especially, when it means transcending the borders of accounting and trespassing into the territories of other disciplines. Cooperation with other disciplines is desirable, but coopting the functions of another discipline to the detriment of one's own discipline is injudicious. Accounting is not the only discipline that has been confronted with this problem. A parallel situation does exist in the field of history. According to Hartwell (1971, p. 7), historians have been criticized by some economists for having failed to formulate a realistic theory of economic growth, but why should the historians be criticized for failing to do what the economists have failed to do.

Financial Accounting: Abstraction of Reality. The major limitation of financial accounting is that it is an abstraction of reality. Abstraction, as observing of particular cases, describing and measuring them, extracting the common characteristics, formulating the general case and ultimately applying this finding to new but related individual cases, is accepted by accountants without reservation. Being an abstraction of the real world, financial accounting does not and cannot portray all aspects of the reporting entity.

> . . . It follows that while a theory may treat adequately certain traits of a group of things which are common to all members of the group, it does not treat *exhaustively* the properties of any one member of such a group. It is a serious error, therefore, to suppose that a theory, which is an abstraction, is an adequate substitute in every context for that of which it is an abstraction, or that it is a falsification. (Cohen and Nagel, 1934, p. 387)

The failure to portray the many dimensions of the entity has been the source of many criticisms. Since these criticisms stem, not from limitations due to deficiency conditions, but from limitations due to boundary conditions in the accounting discipline, accountants have to try doubly hard to alert (educate) the critics of the circumstances. Despite the boundary conditions of accounting some theorists view significant aspects of the decision-making process as an intricate part of financial accounting; but financial accounting information is only an input (inter alia) into the decision-making process. Indubitably, very few accountants, if any, would argue that financial accounting information is the only relevant information used in the decision-making process, despite Hopwood's (1974, p. 166) lament: that the relationship of accounting information to a wider decision process has only been superficially acknowledged. Nevertheless, there are those theorists who insist on internalizing the decision process which is unequivocally external to financial accounting. Accordingly, internalizing externalities is the next area to be examined.

Attempting to Internalize Externalities

Sub-theories which attempt to internalize externalities (Chambers, 1966, pp. 201-202; Sterling, 1970a) do not make the distinction between the generation of information for decision-making and the criteria for decision-making. To incorporate market signals into financial accounting information (to use opportunity cost as the value of firms' assets) is similar to placing a lighthouse on a moving ship, or placing a landmark on a moving truck. Under such circumstances, neither the lighthouse nor the landmark can serve its intended function — a location point.

On the other hand, the use of replacement cost (the use of incremental cost as the value of firms' assets) is to substitute the consequence(s) of a past decision with the possible financing requirement of a future decision. The use of replacement cost is predicated upon the need to maintain physical capital. However, the maintenance of physical capital in a money economy is not an imperative, but simply one alternative among three alternatives: (a) increase physical capital; (b) maintain physical capital; and (c) reduce physical capital. Whereas, the maintenance of nominal money capital is an imperative, since the recovery of nominal money invested underlies the investment decision. Evidently, the replacement cost approach preempts the managerial decision-making process by preselecting a decision.

The current cost approach (Edwards and Bell, 1961, p. 98), using the cost of replacing existing assets in the second hand market or of reproducing the assets in a similar condition, represents an 'if' proposition — a marginal situation and not a consequence of a past decision. Edwards and Bell (1961, p. 23) recognized the decision situation: "A recognition of individual price changes is necessary to help make the expansion decision. A consideration of the effects of relative price movements might reveal that contraction promises the greatest benefit to stockholders." Though they insist (1961, p. 17): "[t]he overriding function to be served by...[accounting] records is the evaluation of past decisions...[Yet they state], we shall now argue, it is a record of individual price changes that should be incorporated into the accounts."

The objective of using current cost in the determination of current operating performance (the physical capital maintenance approach) is to insure the self-sufficiency of internal financing of future investment plans. Self-sufficiency of internal financing of future investments is a desirable managerial policy, which is not, hereby, being challenged, but it is not an imperative. The use of current cost in the determination of the consequences of past decisions preempts the role of the capital market, whose function it is to allocate money capital to new projects (including potential entrants into an industry) on the basis of prospective returns, not on the basis of retrospective returns. Then, why should marginal conditions, which are used to project prospective returns on new decisions, be the determinants of the retrospective returns on past decisions? The only plausible answer: to insure the retention of funds for future financing requirements.

Although Edwards and Bell (1961, p. 162) do recognize that the expense from asset consumption is not related to the replacement of the asset, yet they maintain that the functions of current cost measure of performance are to provide: (1) a measure of current operating profit which would serve as a guide to potential entrants into an industry (1961, p. 104), and as a guide to asset replacement (1961, p. 224); (2) information to aid management in making better decisions in an uncertain future (1961, p. 271); and (3) management with information so that funds needed for asset replacement are not distributed unknowingly.

In connection with (1), decisions to enter an industry are not based upon past measures of performance but upon projected measures of performance — prospective revenues less prospective costs; if sunk costs should exist, it operates to the benefit of the entity. With regard to (2), the current cost measure relates to the past, it is not really relevant to management assessment of the future. Management assessment of the future includes expectations of price and cost movements, labor and capital markets conditions, etc. Current cost is a hybrid; it is neither a measure of the past nor a projection of the future. With regard to (3), management is fully cognizant of the nominal money flows within the organization, using the recoverable cost approach. The evidence on management's awareness and ability to provide for internal financing of future investment plans is convincing (Brittain, 1966; Donaldson, 1961; Kuh, 1962; Lintner, 1949; and Rumelt, 1974).

Financial accounting information is a constant which interacts with other variables (market signals) to confront decision-makers. The basic equations of financial accounting (a descriptive system) are the axioms for a deductive system: managerial accounting. It is through the recoverable cost approach that these equations are able to faithfully state the actual structure or relationship in the socio-economic system (environment). Therefore, to alter the basis of the constant (the recoverable amount of a sum of money invested) *by incorporating the nature of the change* into the system is to *destroy the information on the structure* of the system. Knowledge of the structure (the feedback information on committed finance) necessary for respecification of the predictive model and knowledge (via managerial accounting) of the nature of the change in conditions (marginal conditions in the use of money) affecting the structure are necessary for decision-making (Marschak, 1974, p. 299; Dobbs, 1940, p. 6).

At times, it is held that the ultimate decision of the decision-maker should be predictable based upon the information which is intended to produce certain decisions.

> Improvements in financial statements (the channel) present problems closely related to the articulation between the accounting Model and the Decision Rule, and to an understanding of the process by which the reader of financial statements goes about decoding them.
>
> It would seem intuitively sensible to suggest that this problem might fruitfully be approached on a normative basis, i.e., how *should* financial statements be prepared, how *should* a person be trained to read them, and what class of decisions *ought* he to make? (Crandall, 1969, p. 465)

In the case of law, the difficulty posed by this proposition is fairly obvious. Given the notions of a formally rational system of justice, conflicting roles would result if the attorneys who presented the case served as the jury and then acted as the judge. In the context of financial accounting, there exist: (1) the accountant who presents what he/she considers to be the facts based upon the accounting rules; (2) the financial analyst who interprets these facts; and (3) the investor who passes judgment, that is decides to commit his/her savings based upon his/her perception and choice of risk/return preference.

It is quite true that the decision-maker at times may use an incorrect or an inadequate prediction model for transforming relevant information. Despite that situation, to incorporate the decision rule into the accounting model clearly would usurp the function of the market place. Worst of all, since it is differences in (1) perception and (2) risk/return preference that makes the market, it would seem that the elimination of the investors' decision processes by such usurpation could only have serious repercussions for society.

Fortunately however, the impossibility, if not the folly, of such an undertaking (the incorporation of the decision rule into the financial accounting model) can be appreciated from the following:

> Common experience suggests, and experiment confirms, that a person does not always make the same

> choice when faced with the same options, even when the circumstances of choice seem in all relevant respects to be the same. However, the bulk of economic theory neglects the existence of such inconsistencies; and the best known theories for decision making, . . . base the existence of measurable utility upon a pattern of invariant two-place relations, sometimes called 'preference' and 'indifference'. This raises a difficulty for any attempt to use such theories to describe and predict actual behavior (Davidson and Marschak, 1959, pp. 233-234).

Furthermore, Ashton (1974, pp. 719-732) has aptly pointed out that: "an individual's descriptive model which is captured via experimental techniques may not be the only 'appropriate' representation of the way he (she) utilizes information in making predictions." In discussing Chambers' (1966) work, Larson raises an important point along similar lines:

> The whole process of assessing the relevance relationship between data and decision is a highly complex and problematical affair. To deny our general state of ignorance of how people behave in commercial situations and to assert that there are known criteria of choice in commercial matters constitutes, in my view, a simplistic perception of human decision...
>
> Several problems in the analysis of human decision may impinge upon the process of determining what information is or is not relevant to a decision. There is no clear understanding on the part of the decision-maker, or on the part of anyone else, as to the closeness of fit between the idealistic decision model and the surrogate decision model that the decision-maker actually uses. Further, the surrogate model, like any surrogate, is not deducible from the decision-maker's general objectives or from the form of an idealized model, even if these are knowable. Accountants may and should engage in expansive research regarding the decision-making function, one result of which might be to discover the extent to which surrogate models are actually used by decision-makers. Perhaps then accountants can determine the form of those models and can provide the necessary informational inputs. How-

> ever, even this is not entirely satisfactory, for we must rest completely upon the decision-maker's ability to pick good surrogate models. . . [T]he decision-model is likely to reflect much more a rationalization of the actual choice than it is to reflect the criteria that played a significant role in the decision. (Larson, 1971, pp. 79-81)

An important point underscoring the preceding statements follows:

> The pragmatic approach to problems in information is yet at the first stage of development. At this stage not only the solution methods but the formulation of the problem itself are arguable. There is nothing surprising in the fact that the parameters of the communication channel (except the case of the statistical measure of information quantity) do not limit themselves the maximum value, but limit it together with the limitations depending on the user (of information). *We consider it to be an interesting conclusion that the declared value of the message proves sometimes unattainable just owing to the properties of the communication channel.* . . (Kulikowski, 1973, p. 71) (Emphasis added)

The conclusion arrived at above is applicable to financial accounting. The decision rule evidently cannot be incorporated into the financial accounting model; the decision device is external to the financial accounting model and is controlled by the decision-maker (user of accounting information). Recognition of the external nature of that fact will insure that no attempt is made to internalize the decision. Furthermore, the decision-maker's decision device is developed in the literature in a sophisticated manner to deal with information in a maximizing fashion.

Information Processing for Decision-Making: Financial Analysis. Marinov and Zhecher (1973, p. 89) have suggested certain iterative algorithms as an adaptive approach by the user of the information to overcome the a priori uncertainty in a Gaussian communication channel. They maintain that exact signal vectors can be determined from current information when processed by means of the suggested algorithms; therefore, optimal decision functions can be determined. Finally, they concluded that the decision-maker could immunize the optimal classification of signals received from the variations in probability characteristics of the communication channel by searching for specific algorithms. Since financial statements constitute a communication channel for the transmission of general (though entity specific) information, the findings of Marinov and Zhecher (1973) are quite relevant. The significance of the foregoing is that it establishes firmly the role of the analysis of financial statements (the search for specific algorithms to immunize the optimal classification of signals received from the variations in the probability characteristics of the communication channel) as differentiated from the role of financial accounting culminating in financial statements (the coding and transmission of signals via a communication channel). The search for specific algorithms characterizes the work of financial analysts.

Given the role of financial accounting information in the capital market, it would seem that the optimal classification of received signals is analyst/investor specific and not information specific. This condition is so because it is the interpretation of information by analysts/investors which accounts for the trading that occurs in the capital market. The capital (securities) market is directly dependent upon different interpretations of the received signals by the participants (Weston, 1967, p. 137); one party who is holding must decide to sell, the other party must have decided to buy — at what price — a compromise. Exchange is impossible in the absence of differences in valuation between buyer and seller. If the two do not interpret the signals (transmitted via financial statements and other sources) differently because of their unique decision devices, or do not receive information from different sources with different emphasis or perspective, there can be no exchange — the entire capital market for that matter will collapse. Speculators are ever present, but then they are limited in acting to offset the decision of an entire investment community. (Bohm-Bawerk, 1973, p. 216; Arrow, 1971, p. 103)

Since: (1) any investor can be a buyer or seller but not both in the same transaction, and (2) the transactions in the market represent a finite scheme, the situation can be pursued using probability theory. When portfolio theory, which is appropriate for decision-making under limited conditions, is used by investors, the role of financial analysis involving financial accounting information in stock selection is virtually nil. However, many decisions are not susceptible or amenable to portfolio theory treatment. For instance, an investor may be desirous of obtaining a better than market return on his/her securities portfolio, in this case the unsystematic risk (the risk inherent in a firm) becomes important. This trade-off between risk and return would increase the need for financial analysis involving financial accounting information. Also, a bank loan to a specific firm, when there is an excess of the supply of funds over the demand for funds, would call for financial analysis using **financial accounting information**. This situation involves the possible future performance of the firm given the possible conditions that could obtain in the economy. In this case, a complete system of n events exist with probabilities $p_1, p_2 \ldots$ $p_i \geq 0$ ($\sum_{i=1}^{n} p_i = 1$) representing a finite scheme (E).

$$E = \begin{pmatrix} E_1 E_2 \ldots E_n \\ p_1 p_2 \ldots p_n \end{pmatrix}$$

Uncertainty and Neutrality. Since "every finite scheme describes a state of *uncertainty*," (Khinchin, 1957, pp. 2-3) the role of financial accounting seems to be as one of a provider of information on the condition which has obtained, in so doing it should reduce uncertainty. Accordingly, accounting reports provide information which reduces uncertainty, but the uncertainty is **unique** to the individual decision-maker. Accordingly, **this uniqueness condition imposes the requirement of neutrality upon financial accounting information**: neutral as to risk-sharing (measurement of the benefits/cost-burden for the purpose of sharing the benefits/cost-burden) to insure equity; and neutral as to the decision process in the sense that the information would be *an aid* in the decision process and *not a determinant* of the decision process (that is a particular decision is not forced upon the decision-maker).

Financial accounting information aids the decision process since the decision-maker's decision device incorporates at least two finite schemes (A, B). For this discussion: A represents the environment (socio-economic conditions), and B represents the operations (organizational posture) of the firm, where p and q are the probabilities.

$$A = \begin{pmatrix} A_1 A_2 \ldots A_n \\ p_1 p_2 \ldots p_n \end{pmatrix} \qquad B = \begin{pmatrix} B_1 B_2 \ldots B_m \\ q_1 q_2 \ldots q_m \end{pmatrix}$$

$$k = 1 \ldots n \qquad\qquad L = 1 \ldots m$$

These two schemes are independent, although they interact — healthy performance (operations) within a poor environment; poor performance (operations) within a healthy environment. These two sets of events $A_k B_L$ ($1 \leq k \leq n$, $1 \leq L \leq m$) with probabilities π_{kL} represent another finite scheme, which is the product of the two (A and B) and designated by AB. The probability π_{kL} of the joint occurrence of the events A_k and B_L is $p_k q_L$ (Khinchin, 1957, p. 8). It would seem that market price in the capital market is a function of the sophisticated analysis of the information available relating to the realization of the two finite schemes A and B. Such information serves as a basis for projecting into the future.

A Monistic View of Accounting Measurement. Unmistakably, the decision process involves the use of financial accounting information, but the decision-device (rule) is external to financial accounting. The decision-device is highly personalized and, therefore, unique to the individual. Despite this condition, it appears that Chambers (1966) and Sterling (1970a) attempt to internalize the decision rule in financial accounting by focusing on a measure for specifying a decision choice from among a given set of alternatives. Under certain circumstances (e.g. investment companies), values for financial accounting produced in accordance with the decision rule (which has a significant role in managerial accounting) can result in financial reporting based on current exit values, the usefulness of which cannot be denied. However, if it is recognized that the specifying of decision variables for the selection among alternatives is a function of managerial accounting, and measurement of performance is the function of financial accounting, while the evaluation of such performance is a function of managerial accounting (qua financial analysis), then it would appear that current exit value is simply a decision variable and is a means of measuring performance in *unique* circumstances. This situation (current exit value as a measure of performance) is a rare and special case; accordingly, it is not the general case. To generalize from this case leads to a monistic view of accounting; and the unfortunate consequence is that the distinction between financial and managerial accounting becomes blurred. Blurring of the distinction between financial and managerial accounting leads to confusion at best, and to condemnation of financial accounting at worst.[7]

Edwards and Bell (1961, pp. 220-227, 272-279) and Edwards, Bell and Johnson (1979, pp. 18-25) make no distinction between the roles of financial accounting and managerial accounting. Their model (replacement cost/current cost) is considered at this time since it is a variant of the Limperg model as given in Mey, (1966), which takes a monistic approach to accounting: decision-making information is considered as appropriate and uniquely sufficient for general purposes.

Implicitly, Chambers (1966, pp. 200-218, 244, 351) eliminates the role of managerial accounting, since he maintains that the rules of the game call for exit values. The same can be said about Sterling (1970a, pp. 157-173) who, though recognizing the role of managerial accounting in the "analysis of alternative valuation methods," concluded "that current exit values are the magnitudes most relevant to commonly encountered decision situations, and the last magnitudes whose reporting should be sacrificed in the event of limited channel capacity." Chambers' (1966, pp. 102, 104) position to a certain extent reflects an amalgamation of the **state of being** and the **possibility of becoming**. The **state of being** should be viewed as captured by financial accounting (measurement of past performance and information on resources and obligations). The **possibility of becoming** should be viewed as captured by managerial accounting (evaluation of past performance for future projection).

> 4.42 *Accounting is a systematic method of retrospective and contemporary monetary calculation the purpose of which is to provide a* **continuous source** *of financial information as a guide to future action in markets*. (Chambers, 1966, p. 102) (Emphasis added)

[7]The failure of accounting as described by Cole (1985, p. 102) focuses on the limitation of financial accounting; no consideration is given to the role of managerial accounting. Quite lamentable is the situation reported by Kaplan (1984, pp. 409-410).

A similar approach to the amalgamation of financial and managerial accounting is to be found in Edwards and Bell (1961):

> ...[J]ust as management uses such [managerial accounting] data primarily for purposes of evaluation, most external uses involve similar evaluations. It should not be surprising then if the same set of [financial] accounting principles can be used to develop [managerial accounting] data suitable to external as well as internal users.'' (Edwards and Bell, 1961, p. 5)

Sub-Theories: Experimentation and Classification

Although being aware of the problems of simplification, Chambers' (1966, p. 91; 1975, p. 59) amalgamation may be due to oversimplification.[8] However, **no attempt is made in this paper to deny the importance of experimentation along the lines proposed by Chambers** (1966, pp. 5-6):[9]

---

[8]Chambers (1966) recognizes the long run but he insists that only the short run is relevant—pp. 204-205. He recognizes the importance of asset mix, yet he insists that only the current cash equivalent is relevant—pp. 197-198. He insists that business operations are capable of the same exit and entry rapidity as are financial assets—securities which are not constrained by complementarity—pp. 200-201.

According to Harrod (1973, p. 77): ''It is one thing to buy a security that can be sold, admittedly perhaps at a loss, in a capital market, and another to embody capital disposal [money] in a specific type of plant which can be redeemed only when that plant sweats out its output over a term of years.''

In effect Chambers entire approach reflects a spot economy, and even in a spot economy future expectations **based upon plans as executed** do enter the picture. See Hicks (1939, pp. 154-160). Also Kosh, (1950, p. 355).

Current exit value is a short run orientation. According to Lowe (1965, p. 48), the short run is not the proper horizon for calculation in an industrial economy characterized by large fixed costs, highly specific and indivisible capital stock.

[9]The role of experimentation in the natural and social sciences is fairly well established. Advances in science have been as a result of discovery by accident and discovery through experimentation.

DIAGRAM 1
THE INVESTMENT DECISION: A MANAGERIAL ACCOUNTING PERSPECTIVE

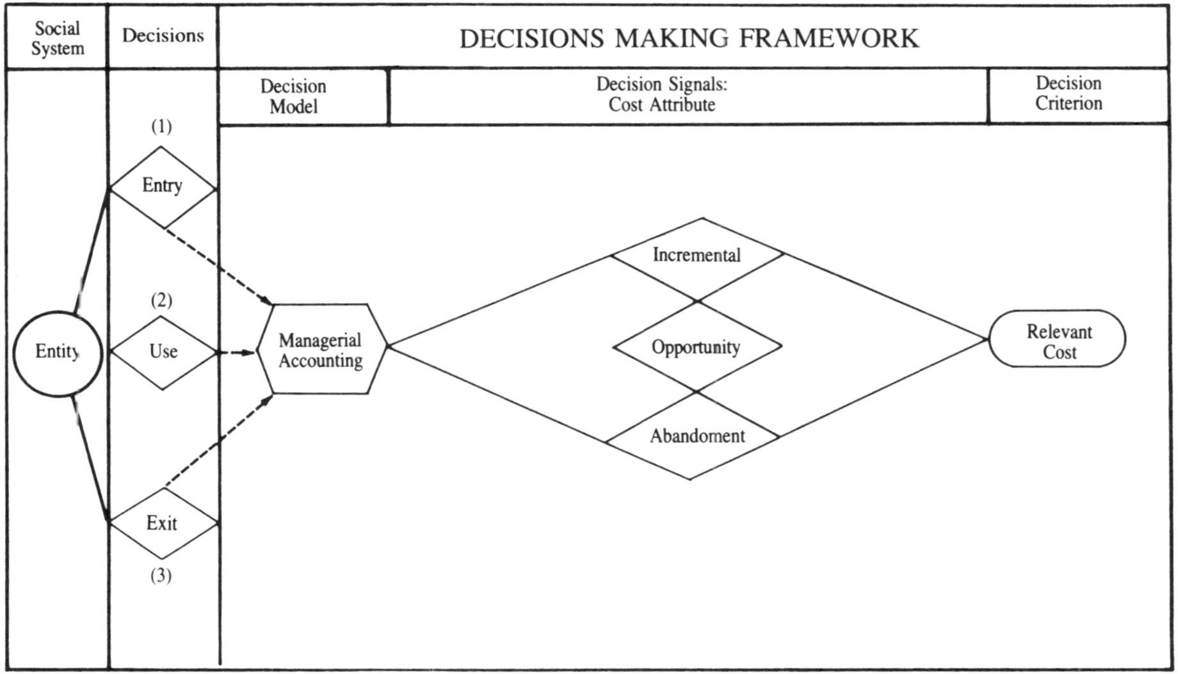

(1) Entry Decision: Replacement Value vs Incremental Cost = Cost of Replacing and /or Expanding Plant Facilities
(2) Use Decision (Discounted Cash Flow): Present Value vs Opportunity Cost = Best Alternative Foregone
(3) Exit Decision: Realizable Value vs Abandonment Cost = Recoverable Cost From an Existing Revenue Stream

> One should be free to imagine rules which have not yet been tried . . . .[*R*]*ules depend on knowledge of their qualities in relation to the condition in which they are expected to work* . . .
> . . . . . . [The] *method by which accounting may be studied* . . . *is not the overt features of the environment in which possible rules are to apply* . . . [T]his method proceeds from propositions which are fundamental inasmuch *as they relate to the conditions which a set of rules must satisfy*. (Emphasis added).

In conclusion of this phase of the analysis, it cannot be overemphasized that the models developed by Limperg, Chambers and Sterling (among others) have demonstrated the generative nature of accounting. Since the main focus of their models is on decision making their contributions fit into the managerial accounting reference file of the library of quantifications (see Diagram 1). Diagram 1 is the author's conception of the relevant cost concept. The relevant cost is the decision-criterion within the decision making framework. Each entity is faced with three decisions: (1) entry; (2) use; and (3) exit. The relevant cost is not some specific predetermined cost; it depends upon the decision. The models discussed above reflect the relevant cost concept for entry and exit decisions. It is clear that these models are very useful in specifying alternatives under specific conditions. Accordingly, these major sub-theories are fully integrable into a general theory of accounting. The following section now sets out to undertake such a task.

IV

The Integration Of The Sub-Theories Into A General Theory

Among the various sub-theories valuation has appeared to be the point of crystallization: the knitting together of all the exchanges between each proposed model and its function. If valuation has this virtue of forcing theorists to develop new models of measurability, it is simply because valuation is at the center of accounting and financial reporting.

The models that theorists uncover by analysis and synthesis are simply combinatory possibilities which are limited to conjoining and disjoining of information. However, in moving back and forth between analysis and synthesis, on returning from decision-making processes to risk-sharing arrangements, there emerges a problem which tends to eliminate the univision structure of financial accounting. **The upsurge of disclosure (expansion of the information base to accommodate dual needs) makes clear that it is the totality of accounting (financial and managerial) and not merely financial accounting that is required to fulfill the financial reporting requirement.** Accordingly it is this development which makes explicit the accounting duality as depicted in Diagram 2.

The Totality of Accounting

Diagram 2 depicts the author's conception of the totality of accounting as a composite of two models—financial accounting and managerial accounting. The two models are shown to be complementary.

Abstraction of Reality: A Closed System Approach. *Financial accounting* focuses on an *abstraction* of reality. It may be thought of as a *closed system* approach with the entity being

DIAGRAM 2
THE DUALISTIC MODEL IN ACCOUNTING: THE TOTALITY OF ACCOUNTING

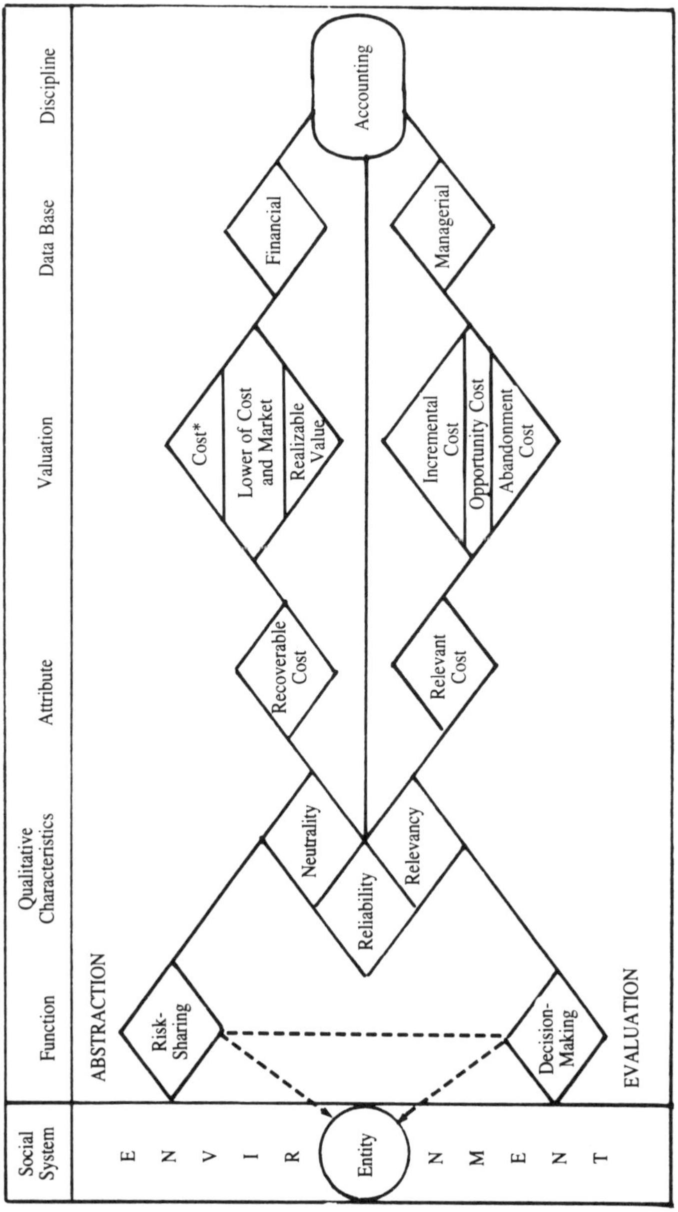

*Dollars Invested

viewed as a self-contained unit adjusting its input and output in response to stimulus from its environment. In this situation articulation is important to insure the interconnectedness of the network of the system. The emphasis is on *control* for *risk-sharing* arrangements (how large is the benefit or the cost burden? how is the benefit or cost burden to be shared?) among the resource providers. The qualitative characteristics of this model are: (1) *reliability* to insure consistency in the determination of the amount of the benefit or burden; and (2) *neutrality* to insure equitable distribution of net income to those who provide resources to a business, or to insure "the distribution of the cost burden among taxpayers and service recipients of a government." (National Council on Governmental Accounting, 1982, para. 66)

The recoverability of the money provided by investors in a business underlies their decision to invest; hence **recoverable cost** (money committed) is the attribute measured. In the case of a governmental unit, budgeted expenditures to provide services to constituents must be financed by revenues to be raised from resource providers (many categories of which will not receive services in proportion to the resources they provide and have no expectation of any return of their "investment"). Owing to the **heterogeneity** of resources, recoverable cost depends on the resource form; accordingly, recoverable cost appears in three states: (a) cost (original money invested); (b) lower of cost and market; and (c) realizable value. For instance in the case of the "lower of cost and market," when market conditions indicate revenue to be generated will not permit full recovery of the money committed, a writedown is necessary to reflect that situation. In the case of a profit-seeking entity, a *loss* is reflected on the books of accounts.

Evaluation of Alternatives: An Open System Approach. *Managerial accounting* focuses on an *evaluation* of alternatives. It may be thought of as an *open system* approach with the entity being viewed as an agent of change. It has the capacity to produce some change in its environment (e.g., increase in advertising to induce customers to increase purchases or influence a change in consumer taste). In this situation cognition is important to insure that the entity is aware of the possibilities and their impact. The emphasis is on *planning* for *decision-making* (how to create the economic or societal benefits? what risks are involved? what risks are to be accepted?) by the management of the entity. The qualitative characteristics of this model are: (1) *reliability* to insure the validity of the plan to create the economic or societal benefits; and (2) *relevancy* to insure that only those factors that affect, or can affect, the plan are evaluated. The **relevant cost** is the attribute given attention. Owing to the **heterogeneity** of decisions, the relevant cost depends on the decision at hand. There are three basic decisions: entry, use and exit; accordingly, the relevant cost appears in three states: (a) incremental cost; (b) opportunity cost; and (c) abandonment cost.

The Relevance Test. The integration of the sub-theories into the general theory is based on a fundamental notion that accounting encompasses an hierarchy of valuations: accounting in its entirety is generative and as such can be viewed as a library of quantifications. Many theorists implicitly accept this proposition. (Mattesich, 1964, p. 231; Vatter, 1945, pp. 512-516). However, it would appear that some theorists (Chambers, 1966, pp. 197-198; Sterling, 1970a, pp. 358-360; 1967, p. 541; Mey, 1966) by assuming several frames of reference for all valuations, rather than isolating the context in which any one valuation should be used, abandon this affirmation (of the library of quantifications). They submit all valuations to the same 'relevance test'; a test which has succeeded at the decision making level, where one is dealing (in the case of each specific decision) with limited decision specific data and a closed set of circumstances (what is to be considered relevant and therefore interpretable in light of the decision in question).

The question which emerges is whether all valuations are homologous. However, the duality of accounting casts doubts upon that possibility.

The Dualistic Model of Accounting

This monograph is based upon the idea that the dualistic model of accounting enables (1) the generation and communication of knowledge pertaining to a specific system—an abstraction of a system by means of financial accounting, and (2) the generation and communication of decision-specific (evaluated) data by means of managerial accounting. The hierarchy of valuations in the field of accounting is derived from the linking of economics, finance and statistics.

The linking of methods, points of views, and models are necessary because accounting as an administrative information science draws from the environment which it serves. Accounting as an administrative information science is a coherent and systematically developed body of knowledge: through financial accounting it permits of a collection of observational data in a manner which describes in a unidimensional manner the behavior of units in markets; and through managerial accounting it permits of mathematical deductions on the observational data of financial accounting. This linking is to be found in the use of the terms incremental cost, opportunity cost, abandonment cost, replacement value, present value and realizable value as illustrated in Diagram 1. These valuations are not exhaustive; there are other strategic valuations, such as probabilistic valuation (Morgenstern, 1963, pp. 74-85) which has a role in managerial accounting. However, the internal linking of probable values presents another problem (Churchman, 1961, pp. 128-129) which would require another type of investigation other than the point estimate for financial accounting under discussion.

The six terms enumerated above are the integrating mechanism of the sub-theories by means of the dualistic model to produce the library of quantifications which is in effect the general theory. The necessary assumptions underlying the general theory to achieve the integration are enumerated below.

The Assumptions Underlying the General Theory

The following assumptions underlie the general theory of accounting as herein presented:

(1) Accounting is a discipline for an empirical science, which consists of the role and primacy of observation, and the subordination of individual occurrences to a generalized model (a classification schema). In a money economy, financial accounting provides a ranking through values determined by monetary exchange.

The possibility of constituting accounting as a specific field of a science was advanced by Sombart (Most, 1979, p. 262), who drew the distinction between accounting and administration. Everything which pertains to accounting falls, in effect, within the same domain; while administration being dispersed among the domains of psychology, sociology, political science, physiology, etc., cannot constitute a unique field of a specific discipline. By relegating to administration the psycho-physiological execution, the individual performance, and the free combinations of decision variables, Sombart reserves to accounting the rules which constitute the code for information acquisition and dissemination to the organizational community — "the central propensity structure". The organizational community (the central propensity structure) is characterized by a collection of administrators among whom the choice of the free combinations of decision variables is a critical function. In financial accounting, a homogeneous attribute is isolated; that attribute is the recoverable amount of a sum of money invested, since recoverability of the money outlay at the minimum (e.g., the payback period criterion) underlies the investment decision in a money economy. "In governmental units there is an implicit contractual understanding that the cost of providing services will be recovered from contributions of taxpayers, grantors and service recipients." (National Council on Governmental Accounting, 1982, para. 48)

(2) Within accounting itself it is necessary to distinguish between: (a) a science of states of system — a synchronic theory of financial accounting, in which case each balance sheet represents a **state of being**; and (b) a science of changes — a diachronic theory of managerial accounting, in which case it is the ability to produce change: **the possibility of becoming**.[10]

Change, as used in the science of changes, signifies "the passage from one state of system to another";[11] unequivocally, understanding is achieved by arranging the elements in a simultaneous grouping — signal information (Marschak and Radner, 1972, pp. 47, 52, 183).

The difference between sychronic and diachronic is that synchronic is time dependent: eventual; whereas diachronic is atemporal: potential. In purely synchronic terms, valuation (value) at any given moment has more than one measure; however the multiple measures belong to the same state of system. Yet, for a state of being, no single measure of value transcends the other values. However, owing to the primacy of the function: a description of the state of being for the purpose of

[10] The concepts of diachronic and synchronic changes are borrowed from Ricoeur (1974, pp. 68, 81, 84).

[11] For an extension of the decision process and the independence of the state of the system, see Radner (1972, p. 15).

risk sharing, (e.g. the financial condition, results of operations), the recoverable cost as the single value makes financial accounting valuation a *cumulative* process.

As a displaceable value, recoverable cost survives the transitory instance of decision-making and remains available for new uses. It provides a continuous history because of the ability of use without leaving or destroying the system. Accordingly, financial accounting valuation is capable of being assigned new dimensions of measure (new values through managerial accounting for assessing the possibilities of becoming) without losing the old value. It is the cumulative process, the nominal money commitments in resources and obligations as embodied in financial accounting information, which is projected throughout the markets of the socio-economic system. The cumulative process is the result of a plan arrived at based upon economic analysis and evaluations and projections developed through managerial accounting. In diachronic terms, managerial accounting pursues a change from a state of being (an existing set of conditions and results) to another preferred state of being (a preferred set of conditions and results). The pursuit of change entails an investigation of the possibility of becoming — projection of expected actualization by reference to choice and innovation.

(3) In a given state of a system absolute terms are not relevant, only relative terms are relevant (i.e., exchange value productivity). Accounting is not an end but a means. Therefore, if the intelligible means par excellence (of financial accounting) is the expressing of claims and resources which can be interpreted as potentialities: controllables which are revenue generators, then one should only consider the relative measures (e.g. the rate of return on money invested or the budget surplus or deficit in relation to total costs) and the negative and opposite relationships with respect to each other (e.g. Debt/Asset ratio) as a meaningful interpretation of the state of being as of a given date.

(4) Articulation of financial accounting data must be maintained as a closed system in order to permit analysis — syntactic information. It is posited that economic rationality is at the center of a closed system of data; thus financial accounting theory, though not managerial accounting, can consider that the entity, the system which it exteriorizes, in the form of financial statements has only internal relations.

(5) The definition of information which satisfies the preceding four assumptions provides a departure from the assumption that all information is decision specific. Given the social function of financial accounting as an institutional arrangement for risk-sharing in an economic undertaking, be it the pursuit of profits or societal benefits, the danger in defining information as being **only** decision specific data is to establish a phenomenology of decision-making in opposition to an information science of accounting.

Information Science and the Phenomenology of Decision-Making

The following position is characteristic of a phenomenology of decision-making: "The [accounting] profession ought to tell the receivers which decision theories are correct and then supply the data specified by those theories." (Sterling, 1970b, p. 455)

As indicated earlier, accounting permits management to control its resources, plan its activities, and evaluate its results. These functions are accommodated in a complementary manner by the duality of accounting. To treat accounting as "a part of the more general decision theories" or as being "constructed from the specifications of the broader theories of economic decisions" (Sterling, 1970b, pp. 456-457) is to reduce accounting drastically from information science to a mere statistics gathering system: "Accounting figures are simply measurement inputs to the decision theories." (Sterling, 1970b, p. 456) Both Mattesich (1964) and Mock (1971) have dealt with the issue of information as it relates to accounting and have shown that accounting information is far broader than mere input for decision-models.

It would seem that since there is an overlap between information generation and decision-making, it would be economical to join the two functions. However, since all information generated is not decision-making oriented, then the purpose of information generation is not identical with decision-making. (Arrow, 1974, p. 58) It is the narrow decision view of financial accounting information as information generated for decision-making which gives rise to an apparent antinomy in accounting between information generating processes and decision-making processes. The antinomy is only apparent since the concept of the library of quantifications permits both decision-making data models and general information generating models to exist in a complementary fashion. Furthermore, the emergence of new models, which involve the generation of accounting information that is situational and critical to insure the purposefulness of accounting, merely reflects the generative aspect of accounting.

The models discussed in this monograph and related models can be set up according to an hierarchy of valuations.

An Hierarchy of Accounting Valuations

An hierarchical level of accounting valuations is depicted in Table 1, a discussion of which is presented below. Within the framework of the library of quantifications, there exist: (1) a calculus for decision-making, present value; and (2) a calculus for risk-sharing, realized return (derived benefit).

Following the reasoning of Reichenbach (1963, pp. 240-241), the present value of an uncertain future benefit stream is a posit: "a statement which we treat as true although we do not know whether it is so." If there are two posits, one with a probability of 80% and another with a probability of 70%, the one with the 80% probability is preferred. However, the degree of probability in no manner attaches any truth to the statement, such a probability merely provides a guide to the selection of a posit (e.g. the expected value). Such a guide is necessary for decision-making.

On the other hand, the realized return (derived benefit) is a more certain proposition since it is determined from past events; its uncertain feature is in the recoverable cost. However, financial accounting gives due cognizance to the current and expected conditions, and the uncertainty is reduced to a minimum. Such an approach is necessary for determining the size of the benefit or the cost burden and how it can be shared. Risk sharing arrangements among the suppliers of resources (creditors and stockholders of businesses, or taxpayers and other resource providers of governments) are accommodated in this setting.

Having viewed the calculi, the different valuations are to be examined in light of their significance or functions. Since use of an asset and exit out of an asset are not possible before entry into that asset, one finds entry value at the top of the hierarchy. Entry value rules govern asset acquisition: incremental cost vs incremental revenue. Anytime after entry, the management can exit: decide to sell since the decision was in error or circumstances have changed. Exit value rules govern asset retention: abandonment cost (the

TABLE 1
ACCOUNTING: A LIBRARY OF QUANTIFICATIONS

	MARKET DICHOTOMY	
Transaction/Events	Spot (Financial)	Forward (Production)
	Accounting Dualism	
Information	MANAGERIAL	FINANCIAL
Purpose	Planning (Decision-Making)	Control (Risk-Sharing)
Calculus	Prospective (Feedforward) Present Value of Future Transactions Discounting Process	Retrospective (Feedback) Derived Benefit on Past Transactions Compounding Process
Variables	Decision: 1) Incremental Cost Entry Value (Replacement Value) 2) Opportunity Cost Exit Value (Realizable Value) 3) Abandonment Cost Use Value (Amount that would not be recovered if the operating plan is abandoned)	Performance: 1) Investment Cost/Cost Burden Recoverable Cost (The Recoverable Amount of a Sum of Money Invested) 2) Benefit as Reflected by Rate of Return on Investment or Rate of Redistribution of Income 3) Risk/Benefit Exposure Risk as reflected in resource and finance portfolios of the entity

future benefit stream) vs realizable value (the current benefit from disposal). Use of assets is according to a plan; clearly use value rules govern asset utilization: present value of a plan (discounted cash flow of one plan) vs opportunity cost (the discounted cash flow of alternative plans).

A change in the hierarchical level of accounting valuation occurs when there is a need to move from risk-sharing calculation to a planning calculation due to a new condition created by the market forces. This new condition is not part of accounting theory but of decision theory. By changing the focus of the governing theory, one also changes the function of the information — a movement from financial accounting to managerial accounting. From a planning perspective the financial accounting concept of recoverable cost is essentially the same as the managerial accounting concept of abandonment cost. This shift provides the opportunity of experiencing accounting information as evaluated data.

The Apparent Antinomy in Accounting. The market forces include all the traits that underlie the apparent antinomy in accounting with financial accounting as a risk-sharing (stewardship and organizational performance) structure and managerial accounting as a planning events framework (e.g. abandonment cost versus opportunity cost). The market forces (be it unemployment that affects governmental tax revenues or business sales revenues, or any of many other factors) attest that this antinomy is not real, since both risk-sharing and decision-making data models are needed. Thus, the apparent antinomy is at the heart of accounting dualism:

(1) Managerial accounting (decision-making) is viewed as an active process which emphasizes the possibility of becoming. To decide is a present event, a transitory, ephemeral act. Financial accounting (risk-sharing), on the other hand, is extemporal for it expresses the gestation of plans over successive time periods, a sort of financial kinetic energy: expended effort, the consequences—results and residues. This condition is referred to as a state of being. Financial accounting only intimates future service potential. Given management's future plans, financial accounting information is only a starting point for determining existing capability; thus, any additional requirements for plan fulfillment can be projected, and the feasibility of such plans can be evaluated via managerial accounting.

(2) Decision-making involves a series of alternatives for which certain acceptable risks are accepted and others rejected. In managerial accounting (event or cause orientation), **choice** (alternative) is the main focus of attention. In financial accounting (structure or result orientation), **constraint** (recoverable amount of investment) is the corresponding counterpart.

(3) The alternatives generated by managerial accounting information produce new combinations, new market forces and new consequences. The virtually infinite generation of new decisions in managerial accounting has as its counterpart in financial accounting a finite and closed collection of results.

Accounting Duality in a Systems Context

The implication of the foregoing discussion can be better appreciated through two systems: (1) a closed system for financial accounting, and (2) an open system for managerial accounting. Table 2 presents the two systems view of accounting.[12]

All of the values are used in accounting at the appropriate time; therefore, there is no monistic approach to valuation in accounting. At each decision point the appropriate decision variables are selected by the decision maker. Abandonment cost would always be compared with opportunity cost. Since the acquisition of an asset was based upon carefully developed plans, if a plan as executed is profitable it invariably costs more to abandon and seize a new opportunity than it does to continue once the plan has been set in motion. If the implemented plan is not cost-effective and is simply a drain on resources, the plan will be abandoned because the opportunity cost will be more than the abandonment cost. As long as risk-sharing arrangements of economic undertakings among the various members of society are expressed in monetary terms, abandonment cost must be considered. It is only through the completion of the plan that social benefits of the plan can be derived, thereby permitting a redirection of money to the creation of social benefits in other areas; or in the case of user fees, that the

[12]The importance of accountants explicating the accounting duality in a systems context cannot be overemphasized. Such an explication, hopefully, would have precluded an unnecessary condemnation of financial accounting in a very prestigious journal. (Cole, 1985, p. 102)

TABLE 2

ACCOUNTING: AN ADMINISTRATIVE INFORMATION SCIENCE

<table>
<tr><td colspan="2" align="center">Information Acquisition and Dissemination</td></tr>
<tr><td align="center">OPEN SYSTEM</td><td align="center">CLOSED SYSTEM</td></tr>
<tr><td align="center">MANAGERIAL ACCOUNTING</td><td align="center">FINANCIAL ACCOUNTING</td></tr>
<tr><td><u>Planning/Feedforward</u>
Evaluation Orientation - Constructing and Testing (using feedback)
Incremental Cost (1)
Entry Value - Replacement Value
Opportunity Cost (2)
Exit Value - Realizable Value
Abandonment Cost (3)
Use Value - Planned Value/Use Expectation
Decision Orientation - Financing and Investing
Liquidity Cost and
Collateral Value</td><td><u>Control/Feedback</u>
Observation Orientation - Operating and Learning (using feedforward)
Matching (A defined operation for measuring organizational performance)
Identification of Benefits and Sacrifices
Realization (A quality control measurement condition to insure the quality of of organizational performance)
Critical Event for Determining Admissible Benefits and Sacrifices
Performance Orientation - Operating
Money Committed/Recoverable Cost (3)
Derived Benefit: Return on Investment Redistribution of Income</td></tr>
<tr><td><u>DECISION: EX ANTE CONCEPT</u>
Risk Determination and Acceptance
Discounted Cash Flow of Expected Revenue Stream
= Present Value of Investment
= Ex Ante Sunk Costs</td><td><u>PERFORMANCE: EX POST CONCEPT</u>
Risk Accepted and Benefit Established
Actual Cash Outlay in Implementing the Decision
= Money Committed (Asset Portfolio/Cost Burden)
= Ex Post Sunk Cost</td></tr>
</table>

(1) The Limperg and Edwards and Bell Models (2) The Chambers and Sterling Models

(3) The Conventional Financial Accounting Model

money committed to the plan can be released (and gradually at best) for its employment in another area (Cipolla, 1980, p. 110; Harrod, 1973, p. 77). Financial accounting reflects a plan as constituted in nominal money terms in its progression through time.

Given the dualistic model of accounting, it appears that one can now safely categorize the models proposed by Chambers (1966), Edwards and Bell (1961), Limperg (1919), Mey (1966) and Sterling (1970a). This categorization of the models is implicit in the American Accounting Association Committee's report (1977). In that report, the Committee explicitly recognized that none of the sub-theories was an appropriate general theory and implicitly recognized that they were special cases. However, these models are presented as decision models (Chambers, 1966, pp. 102, 141, 142, 203; Edwards and Bell, 1961, pp. 3, 4, 15; Sterling, 1972), and thus they belong to the realm of managerial accounting rather than financial accounting. In the case of the Limpergian replacement value accounting [the main proponent is Mey (1966)], the decision focus is revealed in Mey (1966, pp. 6, 22, 23):

> The theory of value is applied to the analysis of the internal operations of business organizations. Taking account of all 'necessary' sacrifices at each production centre, it is possible to obtain an analytic representation which is *normative* in character. . . . *Normative costing in this manner is indispensable as an aid in choosing between alternative actions of every kind, and for planning and budgeting*. (Mey, 1966, p. 6) (Emphasis added).

It is necessary at this stage of the discussion to emphasize that the importance of these models is that they constitute the tests by which the financial plan as reflected in financial accounting is to be deemed satisfactory or unsatisfactory by the decision-makers. Table 2 depicts this testing process, which reflects the scientific approach of management.

Accounting Valuation Systems and Management's Scientific Approach

The major criticism of financial accounting stems from the false assumption that decision-making is locked into the valuation used in financial accounting (Journal of Accountancy, 1983)[13] However, the concept of **Accounting as a library of quantifications**, enables a new relation of a nonantinomic character between constraint (risk-sharing: stewardship and performance arrangements) and choice (decision-making: evaluating and selecting among alternatives). Risk-sharing and decision-making are two distinct processes. Behind each of these two processes there exist distinct, though related, systems of valuation. Table 2 shows that financial accounting valuation should not be the basis of the investment decision. The role of financial accounting information as an institutional arrangement for risk-sharing arrangement among the suppliers of resources (creditors and stockholders, or taxpayers, grantors and service recipients) has been hindered because of the misconception.

Following the reasoning developed by Yovits and Ernst (1970, pp. 3, 4, 7, 9, 28, 29) for the purposes of financial accounting, management as the decision-maker is viewed as using the scientific method: a combined deductive and inductive approach. Management develops an hypothesis (a budget-plan of action) that is expected to result in predictable observable actions—monetary exchange as reflected in projected financial statements. The hypothesis (budget) is the basic prediction model of management, and managers hope that the hypothesis (budget) as formulated agrees with the real world (will be achieved). Unequivocally, there must be a way of (1) constructing and (2) evaluating the hypothesis (the budget). Since the hypothetico-deductive method used by management is explanatory induction (managerial accounting), generalizations from observations (financial accounting) constitute the basis for constructing the hypothesis.

Events and transactions, resulting from operating with the external environment over which management has no control, are transformed into data (financial statements). This data along with information about the external environment and other appropriate

[13]For a very good appreciation of this problem see Milliman, (1972, p. 31).

information (the performance of similar firms in the industry and other industry related data) disseminated to management for decision-making purposes enables management to decide (test): (1) whether the budgeting model (hypothesis) used is an accurate model of the operating environment; (2) whether the budgeting model should be modified, discarded; or (3) whether more experimentation or data are needed. The hypothesis formulation and testing is the realm of managerial accounting; whereas financial accounting involves the transformation of transactions/events into data.

In financial accounting one is essentially confronted with intelligible structuralism in terms of information; that is one is dealing with (1) observable phenomena already constituted, and (2) an established inventory of elements (assets, equities, revenues, expenses, gains and losses) which are placed in binary opposition based upon an algebra of these elements: Assets = Equities; Revenues = Expenses + Excess of Revenues (Expenses) over Expenses (Revenues).[14] However, under managerial accounting the system is dynamic, and the planning process permits an infinite combination of elements.

The Legitimacy of Financial Accounting. If financial accounting has some hold on legitimacy, it is on the level of risk-sharing efficiency, the laws of which are inherent in its approach to valuation to arrive at an efficient and equitable basis for risk-sharing among the suppliers of resources. In the case of the governmental unit, recoverable cost is the relevant attribute because the budget surplus or deficit is a signal to management. The recoverable amount of a sum of money invested, in the case of the business enterprise, emerges as the relevant attribute, because exit value is a signal to management. If management chooses to **use** rather than **sell** the assets under its control, it is fairly obvious that the risk accepted and return to be calculated for the purpose of risk-sharing among suppliers of finance can only be based upon the decision to use rather than to sell. Financiers can only share in the actual result, whatever it happens to be.

---

[14] Revenues consist of sales revenues, tax revenues, grants, user fees, miscellaneous gains on disposal of resources, etc. Expenses consist of cost of services provided, grants provided, miscellaneous losses on disposal of resources, etc.

Unequivocally, exit value is a decision variable which management has to consider, and which it does consider within the context of managerial accounting. Once the decision is made to use rather than sell, projection must focus on the benefits from asset's use and not possible gains from asset's sale. Under the conditions of asset's use, the recoverable amount of money is the desired attribute, and it is that attribute which is measured even when current market value is used as in the case of investment companies. The reason for the use of market values in the case of investment companies is simply that the *risk-sharing arrangement calls for the investment companies to sell and redeem their shares at the realizable value at the end of each trading day of the securities portfolio held*. In that situation no use value exists to the investment companies; *the investment companies merely act as an intermediary* (obviously there is the issue of economy of scale in addition to participating in a portfolio) *between the individual investor and the securities market*. In this situation, the recoverable amount is the current market value, since that is the amount that the individual would have received or paid for the holdings, had the individual been trading for his/her own account in the open market.

V

CONCLUSION

The theoretical propositions, emanating from the problem areas examined, appear to be necessary steps along the tedious journey of accounting theory development. The analyzed propositions (the sub-theories solutions to perceived deficiencies in financial accounting theory) have been shown to be useful in a managerial accounting context while failing to satisfy the complex practical ramifications imposed on financial accounting information by the very nature of the socio-economic system.

The four designated categories of sub-theories find their rationale in functional, but partial models of the socio-economic system. They are unequivocally special cases of a general theory of accounting in a system of monetary exchanges. However, the significance of those partial models **should not** be underestimated because of their limited usefulness. Since they are entries in the portfolio of quantifications, they must be viewed as an integral part of a unified general theory of accounting.

Given the increasing need for new perceptions (more breadth and depth in information) of the socio-economic system, accounting in its totality **as a library of quantifications** permits the adaptation of these partial models to satisfy the many varied, **but specific**, uses for information. It seems that the existing financial accounting (recoverable cost) model because of its comprehensiveness would continue as a general purpose information (data) base from which extrapolations shall be made; accordingly, the existing managerial accounting (relevant cost) model because of its evaluative nature would continue as a means of generating specific information (evaluated data), since it permits of mathematical deductions from financial accounting information. The two models would continue to exist in a complementary manner to constitute the totality of the accounting discipline.

BIBLIOGRAPHY

American Accounting Association Committee on Concepts and Standards for External Financial Reports, *Statement on Accounting Theory and Theory Acceptance*. American Accounting Association, 1977.

Arrow, Kenneth J. *The Limits of Organization*. New York: W.W. Norton & Company, Inc., 1974.

———. "The Firm in General Equilibrium Theory." *The Corporate Economy, Growth, Competition and Innovative Potential*. Cambridge, Massaschusetts: Harvard University Press, 1971.

Ashton, Robert H. "The Predictive Ability Criterion and User Prediction Models." *Accounting Review* (October, 1974).

Basmann, R.L. "The Brookings Quarterly Econometric Model: Science or Numbers Mysticism." *Problems and Issues in Current Econometric Practice*. Edited by Karl Brunner. Columbus, Ohio: College of Administrative Science, The Ohio State University, 1972.

Bohm-Bawerk, Eugen von. *Value and Price*, 2nd. Rev. Ed. Illinois: Libertarian Press, 1973.

Beaver, William H.; Kennelly, John W.; and Voss, William M. "Predictive Ability as a Criterion for the Evaluation of Accounting Data." *Accounting Review* (October 1968).

Boyd, Edward. "Ancient Systems of Accounting," *A History of Accounting and Accountants*. Edited and partly written by Richard Brown. New York: Augustus M. Kelley Publishers, 1968. London: Frank Cass and Company Limited, 1st. Ed., 1905.

Brittain, John A. *Corporate Dividend Policy*. Washington, D.C.: The Brookings Institution, 1966.

Canning, John B. *The Economics of Accountancy: A Critical Analysis of Accounting Theory*. New York: The Ronald Press Co., 1929.

Chambers, Raymond J. "NOD, COG and PuPU: See How Inflation Teases." *Journal of Accountancy* (September, 1975).

———. *Accounting, Evaluation and Economic Behavior*. Englewood Cliffs, New Jersey: Prentice-Hall, Inc., 1966.

Churchman, C. West. *Prediction and Optimal Decision: Philosophical Issues of a Science of Values*. Englewood Cliffs, New Jersey: Prentice-Hall, Inc., 1961.

Cipolla, Carlo M. *Before the Industrial Revolution: European Society and Economy, 1000-1700*. Second Edition. New York; London: W.W. Norton & Company, 1980.

Cohen, Morris R. and Nagel, Ernest. *An Introduction to Logic and Scientific Method*. New York; Burlingame: Harcourt, Brace & World, Inc., 1934.

Cole, Robert E. "Target Information for Competitive Performance." *Harvard Business Review* (May-June, 1985).

Crandall, Robert H. "Information Economics and Its Implication for Further Development of Accounting Theory." *Accounting Review* (July, 1969).

Davidson, Donald and Marschak, Jacob. "Experimental Tests of a Stochastic Decision Theory." *Measurement: Definitions and Theories*. Edited by C. West Churchman and Philburn Ratoosh. New York: John Wiley & Sons, Inc.; London: Chapman and Hall, Limited, 1959.

Dobbs, Maurice. *Political Economy and Capitalism: Some Essays in Economic Tradition*. 2nd Edition. London: Routledge & Kegan Paul Ltd., 1940. Reprinted 1960.

Donaldson, Gordon. *Corporate Debt Capacity*. Boston: Harvard University Press, 1961.

Edwards, Edgar O. and Bell, Philip W. *The Theory and Measurement of Business Income*. Berkeley; Los Angeles; London: University of California Press, 1961.

Edwards, Edgar O.; Bell, Philip W. and Johnson, L. Todd. *Accounting for Economic Events*. Houston: Scholars Book Co. 1979.

Eiriksson, Benjamin. *Outline of an Economic Theory*. Reykjavik, Iceland: Helgafell Publishing Company, 1954.

Ellis, Brian. *Basic Concepts of Measurement*. Cambridge, England: Cambridge University Press, 1966.

Enthoven, Adolf J. H. *Accounting and Economic Development Policy*. Amsterdam; London: North Holland Publishing Company. New York: American Elsevier Publishing Company, Inc., 1973.

Friedman, Milton and Schwartz, Anna J. *Monetary Trends in the United States and United Kingdom: Their Relation to Income, Prices and Interest Rates*. A National Bureau of Economic Research Monograph. Chicago and London: The University of Chicago Press, 1982.

Gordon, Barry. *Economic Analysis before Adam Smith: Hesiod to Lessius*. London: The Macmillan Press, Ltd. New York: Harper & Row Publishers, Inc., 1975.

Guerlac, Henry. "Quantification in Chemistry," *Quantification: A History of the Meaning of Measurement in the Natural and Social Sciences*. Edited by Harry Woolf. Indianapolis; New York: The Bobbs-Merrill Company, Inc., 1961.

Hanna, Joseph F. "On the Cognitive Content of Econometric Models," *Problems and Issues in Current Econometric Practice*. Edited by Karl Brunner. Columbus, Ohio: College of Administrative Science, The Ohio State University, 1972.

Harrod, Roy. *Economic Dynamics*. London and Basingstoke: The Macmillan Press Ltd., 1973.

Hartwell, R.M. *The Industrial Revolution and Economic Growth*. London: Methuen & Co., Ltd., 1971.

Hendriksen, Eldon S. *Accounting Theory*. Fourth Edition, Homewood, Illinois: Richard D. Irwin, Inc., 1982.

Hicks, John R. *Value and Capital*. Oxford: The Clarendon Press, 1939.

Hopwood, Anthony. *Accounting and Human Behavior*. Englewood Cliffs, New Jersey: Prentice-Hall, Inc., 1974.

Ijiri, Yuji. "Logic and Sanctions in Accounting." *Accounting in Perspective: Contributions to Accounting Thought by Other Disciplines*. Edited by Robert R. Sterling and William F. Bentz. New Rochelle, New York; Brighton, England; Burlingame, California: South-Western Publishing Company, 1971.

Jensen, Robert E. "Logic and Sanctions in Accounting: Critique." *Accounting in Perspective: Contributions to Accounting Thought by Other Disciplines*. Edited by Robert R. Sterling and William F. Bentz. New Rochelle, New York; Brighton, England; Burlingame, California: South-Western Publishing Company, 1971.

Johnson, Charles E. "Inventory Valuation: The Accountant's Achilles Heel." *Accounting Review* (January 1954) as cited in *Financial Accounting Theory I: Issues and Controversies*. Second Edition. Edited by Stephen A. Zeff and Thomas F. Keller. New York; London; Toronto: McGraw-Hill Book Company, 1973.

Journal of Accountancy. "Inflation-adjusted data: the 'real' corporate profit." (August 1983, pp. 119-120).

Kaplan, Robert S. "The Evolution of Management Accounting." *Accounting Review* (July 1984).

Khinchin, A.I. *Mathematical Foundations of Information Theory*. Translated by R. A. Silverman and M. D. Friedman. New York: Dover Publications, Inc., 1957.

Kosh, David A. "Tangible Assets of Public Utilities." *Studies in Income and Wealth*. Volume Twelve. Conference on Research in Income and Wealth. New York: National Bureau of Economic Research, 1950.

Kravis, Irving B. "Comparative Studies of National Incomes and Prices." *Journal of Economic Literature* (March 1984).

Kuh, Edwin. *Capital Stock Growth: A Micro-econometric Approach*. Amsterdam: North Holland Publishing Company, 1962.

Kulikowski, J. L. "Notes on the Value of Information Transmitted Through a Communication Channel." *2nd. International Symposium on Information Theory*. Edited by B. N. Petrov and F. Csaki. Budapest: Akademiai Kiado, 1973.

Lambert, Maurice. "La naissance de la bureaucratie." *Revue Historique* (TOME DCXXIV, 1960).

Larson, Kermit D. "Are There Commercial Foundations of Accounting Theory?" *Foundations of Accounting Theory*. Edited by Williard E. Stone. Gainesville: University of Florida Press, 1971.

Leibenstein, Harvey. *Beyond Economic Man: A New Foundation for Microeconomics*. Cambridge, Massachusetts; London, England: Harvard University Press, 1976.

Lintner, John. *Corporate Profits in Perspective*. Washington, D.C.: American Enterprise Association, Inc., 1949.

Littleton, A.C. "Factors Limiting Accounting." *Accounting Review* (July 1970).

———. "Prestige for Historical Cost." *Contemporary Studies in the Evolution of Accounting Thought*. Edited by Michael Chatfield. Belmont, California: Dickenson Publishing Company, Inc. 1968.

Littleton, A.C. and Zimmerman, V.K. *Accounting Theory: Continuity and Change*. Englewood Cliffs, New Jersey: Prentice-Hall, Inc., 1962.

Lowe, Adolph. *On Economic Knowledge: Towards a Science of Political Economics*. New York and Evanston: Harper & Row Publishers, 1965.

MacNeal, Kenneth. *Truth in Accounting*. Philadelphia: University of Pennsylvania Press. London: Humphrey Milford, Oxford University Press, 1939.

Marinov, Yu. P. and Zhecher, B. Zh. "On an Adaptive Method of Optimal Signal Classification." *2nd. International Symposium on Information Theory*. Edited by B.N. Petrov and F. Csaki. Budapest: Akademiai Kiado, 1973.

Marion, John B. *Physics: The Foundation of Modern Science*. New York; London; Sydney; Toronto: John Wiley & Sons, Inc., 1973.

Marschak, Jacob. *Economic Information, Decision, and Prediction – Selected Essays: Volume III*. Dordrecht-Holland; Boston: D. Reidel Publishing Company, 1974.

Marschak, Jacob and Radner, Roy. *Economic Theory of Teams*. New Haven; London: Yale University Press, 1972.

Mattessich, Richard. *Accounting and Analytical Methods: Measurement and Projection of Income and Wealth in the Micro- and Macro- Economy*. Homewood, Illinois: Richard D. Irwin, Inc., 1964.

Mey, Abram. "Theodore Limperg and His Theory of Values and Costs." *Abacus* (September 1966).

Milliman, Jerome W. "Beneficiary Charges – Toward a Unified Theory." *Public Prices for Public Products*. Edited by Selma Mushkin. Washington: The Urban Institute, 1972.

Mock, Theodore J. "Concepts of Information Value and Accounting." *Accounting Review* (October 1971).

Moonitz, Maurice. *The Basic Postulates of Accounting*. Accounting Research Study No. 1. New York: American Institute of Certified Public Accountants, 1961.

Morgenstern, Oskar. *On the Accuracy of Economic Observations*. Second Edition. Princeton, New Jersey: Princeton University Press, 1963.

Most, Kenneth S. "Sombart on Accounting History." *Working Paper Series,* Volume 2. Academy of Accounting Historians. Edited by Edward N. Coffman. No City: The Academy of Accounting Historians, Virginia Commonwealth University, 1979.

National Council on Governmental Accounting. *Objectives of Accounting and Financial Reporting for Governmental Units*. Concepts Statement 1. Chicago, Illinois: National Council on Governmental Accounting, 1982.

Page, Frances M., Editor. *Wellingborough Manorial Accounts A.D. 1258-1323 From the Account Rolls of Crowland Abbey*. Kettering: The Northamptonshire Printing & Publishing Company, Ltd., 1936.

Paton, William Andrew. *Accounting Theory*. New York: The Ronald Press, 1922.

Popper, Karl R. *Objective Knowledge; An Evolutionary Approach*. Oxford: The Clarendon Press, 1972.

Radner, Roy. "Normative Theory of Individual Decision: An Introduction." *Decision and Organization: A Volume in Honor of Jacob Marschak*. Edited by C.B. McGuire and Roy Radner. Amsterdam; London: North Holland Publishing Company, 1972.

Reichenbach, Hans. *The Rise of Scientific Philosophy*. Berkeley and Los Angeles: University of California Press, 1963.

Ricoeur, Paul. *The Conflict of Interpretations: Essays in Hermeneutics*. Edited by Don Ihde. Evanston: Northwestern University Press, 1974.

Roebuck, Carl. *The World of Ancient Times*. New York: Charles Scribner's Sons, 1966.

Rumelt, Richard P. *Strategy, Structure and Economic Performance*. Cambridge, Massachusetts: Harvard University Press, 1974.

Shannon, H.A. "The Coming of General Limited Liability." *Essays in Economic History*. Edited by E. M. Caru-Wilson. London: Edward Arnold Publishers Ltd., 1954. Reprinted 1966.

Shwayder, Keith. "A Critique of Economic Income as an Accounting Concept." *Income Theory and Rate of Return*. Edited by J. Leslie Livingstone and Thomas J. Burns. No City: College of Administrative Science, The Ohio State University, 1971.

Stephens, Matthew J. "Opening Pandora's Box of Current Cost." *Financial Executive* (May 1967).

Sterling, Robert R. "Decision Oriented Financial Accounting." *Accounting and Business Research* (Summer, 1972).

———. *Theory of the Measurement of Enterprise Income*. Lawrence; Manhattan; Wichita; London: The University of Kansas Press, 1970a.

———. "On Theory Construction and Verification." *Accounting Review* (July, 1970b).

———. "Conservatism: The Fundamental Principle of Valuation in Traditional Accounting." *Abacus* (December 1967) as cited in *Financial Accounting Theory I: Issues and Controversies*. Second Edition. Edited by Stephen A. Zeff and Thomas F. Keller. New York; London; Toronto: McGraw-Hill Book Company, 1973.

Sweeney, Henry W. *Stabilized Accounting*. Foreword by Roy B. Kester. New York and London: Harper & Brothers Publishers, 1936.

Vatter, William J. "Limitations of Overhead Allocation." *Accounting Review* (April 1945) as cited in *Readings in Cost Accounting Budgeting and Control*. Fifth Edition. Edited by William E. Thomas. Cincinnati; Pelham Manor, New York; and other cities: South-Western Publishing Co., 1978.

Weatherall, M. *Scientific Method*. London: The English Universities Press Ltd., 1968.

Weston, J. Fred. "Sources and Costs of Obtaining Funds." *Profits in the Modern Economy: Selected papers From a Conference on Understanding Profits*.Edited by Harold W. Stevenson and J. Russell Nelson. Minneapolis: University of Minnesota Press, 1967.

Wheeler, John T. "Discussion on Norton Bedford Paper 'Information, Business and Society'."*Foundations of Accounting Theory*. Edited by Williard E. Stone. Gainesville: University of Florida Press, 1971.

Williams, Thomas H. and Griffin, Charles H. *The Mathematical Dimension of Accountancy*. Cincinnati; Chicago; New York; and other cities: South-Western Publishing Co., 1964.

Winjum, James Ole. *The Role of Accounting in the Economic Development of England: 1500-1750*. Center for International Education and Research in Accounting, Monograph No. 6. Illinois: University of Illinois Press, 1972.

———. "Accounting in its Age of Stagnation." *Accounting Review (October 1970)*.

Yovits, Marshall C. and Ernst, Ronald L. "Generalized Information Systems: Consequences for Information Transfer." *People and Information*. Edited by Harold B. Pepinsky. New York; Oxford; Toronto and other major cities: Pergamon Press, 1970.